Chicken Soup for the Soul®

Recipes for Busy Moms

"OOH IT'S SO GOOD!!®"

Jack Canfield and Mark Victor Hansen with

Mr. Food®

Health Communications, Inc.
Deerfield Beach, Florida

www.hcibooks.com
www.chickensoup.com
www.mrfood.com

We would like to acknowledge the following publishers and individuals for permission to reprint the following material.

A Pinch of This . . . A Dash of That . . . Reprinted by permission of M. Mylene English. ©1998 M. Mylene English.

Never Say "Yuck!" Reprinted by permission of Caryl Ginsburg Fantel. ©2006 Caryl Ginsburg Fantel.

Every Mom Is a Working Mom. Reprinted by permission of Ann Morrow. ©2005 Ann Morrow.

Super Mom. Reprinted by permission of Jaye Lewis. ©2005 Jaye Lewis.

Thinking Outside the Box Lunch. Reprinted by permission of Jean Blackmer. ©2006 Jean Blackmer.

In the Bag. Reprinted by permission of Deborah Farmer. ©2003 Deborah Farmer.

If You Build It, They Will Come. Reprinted by permission of M. Mylene English. ©1999 M. Mylene English.

Tortilla Soup Torment. Reprinted by permission of Robin Ehrlichman Woods. ©2005 Robin Ehrlichman Woods.

Full Circle. Reprinted by permission of Ellen Javernick. © 2006 Ellen Javernick.

(Continued on page 186)

Library of Congress Cataloging-in-Publication Data
is on file with the Library of Congress.

Recipes ©2006 Cogin, Inc. All rights reserved.

Photos ©2006 Hal Silverman Studio, Inc.

©2006 Jack Canfield and Mark Victor Hansen
ISBN 0-7573-0404-4

All rights reserved. First printing in China. No part of this publication may be reproduced, stored in a retrieval system or transmitted in any form or by any means, electronic, mechanical, photocopying, recording or otherwise, without the written permission of the publisher.

HCI, its Logos and Marks are trademarks of Health Communications, Inc.

The "Mr. Food" and the "OOH IT'S SO GOOD!!" trademarks and logos and the Mr. Food likeness are the sole and exclusive property of Ginsburg Enterprises Incorporated and are used with express consent. All rights in and to the "Mr. Food" and the "OOH IT'S SO GOOD!!" trademarks and logos and the Mr. Food likeness, including copyright and trademark rights, belong solely to Ginsburg Enterprises Incorporated.

Publisher: Health Communications, Inc.
           3201 S.W. 15th Street
           Deerfield Beach, FL 33442–8190

Cover design by Larissa Hise Henoch
Inside book design by Lawna Patterson Oldfield and Andrea Perrine Brower
Mr. Food editorial direction by Caryl G. Fantel
Food styling by Howard Rosenthal, Joe Peppi, Patty Rosenthal, and Diane Dolley of
  Ginsburg Enterprises Incorporated.

·CONTENTS·

Introduction

*T*oday's busy mom faces very different challenges than mothers did a generation ago, and although times have changed, some things are timeless. The heart and soul of a home is still the kitchen, and what *goes on in* and what *comes out of* the kitchen is the heart and soul of a family. Preparing appetizing, healthy, appealing meals is one of the many challenging tasks moms face today. And, sure, being able to pull into a fast-food, take-out lane or pop another frozen entrée into the microwave can be a life-saver, but when a family sits down for a meal together, the experience feeds more than a hungry stomach.

Having breakfast on the run during the week may be unavoidable, but that doesn't mean you can't start the day with something nutritious and easy to fix. That goes for take-along lunches too. And, with the pressures and stress modern families face today, it's more important than ever to get together around the dinner table to talk about each other's days, celebrate the triumphs and commiserate over the troubles.

Eating at home provides a chance to serve healthier meals and save some money; and *no*, it does not have to be more work for moms! Get the kids involved in planning the menus and preparing the food, and give them responsibilities for cleaning up. Make the experience a learning opportunity that's fun, rather than a chore. Ask them to see how many new foods they can work into the menu each week and how many colors of foods they can eat at one meal. Reading recipes teaches kids fractions, measurements (metrics, too!) and foreign terms. Having a meal together turns into something much more than putting a plate of food on the table.

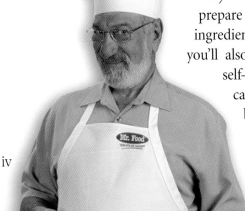

Chicken Soup for the Soul Recipes for Busy Moms will help. You'll find easy-to-prepare dishes that don't require fancy ingredients or special techniques, and you'll also meet women just like yourself—busy moms who are juggling careers, relationships and, well . . . being mom! Come on, join us and enjoy!

Breakfast Pizza

For years you've been telling the kids they can't have pizza for breakfast. We're allowed to change our minds, aren't we? I mean, can you imagine the looks on their faces when you tell them you made pizza for breakfast?!

SERVES 6 to 8

1. Preheat the oven to 450°F.

2. In a large bowl, beat the eggs, salt, pepper, and milk.

3. In a large skillet, melt the butter over medium-low heat. Add the egg mixture and scramble until firm, but not browned.

4. Place the pizza shell on a pizza pan or large cookie sheet and spread the scrambled eggs over the shell; cover evenly with the mushrooms and cheese.

5. Bake for 10 to 12 minutes, until the cheese is melted and the crust is crisp and golden.

Option: *If your gang would prefer, use bell peppers or sliced plum tomatoes instead of the mushrooms, and substitute shredded Cheddar or almost any other cheese that melts well for the mozzarella.*

6 eggs
¼ teaspoon salt
⅛ teaspoon pepper
3 tablespoons milk
1 tablespoon butter
1 (1-pound) store-bought prepared pizza shell, thawed if frozen
1 can (4 ounces) mushroom stems and pieces
½ cup (2 ounces) part-skim mozzarella cheese

Overstuffed Mediterranean Omelet

Forget stopping for a fast-food breakfast! Eggs are one of the fastest foods we can make, and when we team them with fresh veggies and cook 'em in olive oil instead of butter, they're oh-so-good for us!

1 teaspoon olive oil

1 cup fresh baby spinach

¼ cup sun-dried tomatoes, thinly sliced

1 garlic clove, minced

¼ teaspoon salt

3 large eggs, beaten

¼ cup crumbled feta cheese

1 In a small nonstick skillet, heat the oil over medium heat. Add the spinach, sun-dried tomatoes, garlic, and salt. Sauté for 1 minute, or until the spinach is bright green but not wilted; remove the spinach mixture from the skillet and set aside.

2 Add the eggs to the skillet and stir gently for 1 minute; stop stirring and allow the egg to set up for 1 to 2 minutes. Top the eggs with the spinach mixture and sprinkle with the feta cheese. Fold the omelet in half, and serve.

Did You Know . . . *that olive oil can be part of practically any diet, even a low-fat one? It is said to offer protection against heart disease because it helps control LDL ("bad") cholesterol levels while raising HDL ("good") cholesterol levels. Olive oil is also good for us because of its high content of monounsaturated fatty acids and antioxidant substances.*

A Pinch of This . . .
A Dash of That . . .

BY M. MYLENE ENGLISH

*I*t's something I never thought about. It never occurred to me that my cooking style might cause friction in my home, but strange things come to pass, and my relaxed attitude toward cooking has recently come under attack.

My eldest daughter is taking Home Economics at school and is "Learning How to Cook." This would normally be a good thing, but since I am not one to measure or to follow a recipe to the letter, this "Learning How to Cook" is becoming a problem.

My daughter has been "cooking" most of her life. The preparation of food is not something any of my children are strangers to. My daughter uses the stove and the oven and turns out fine meals and snacks. She is now, however, being taught to pay attention to things like measurement and cooking time—things her mother is less than strict about. Her homework assignment last week was to prepare and serve four meals for her family. What followed was absolute torture.

Meal #1: It all began with pancakes on the first morning. My daughter was following the recipe in the book—using the correct measuring cups for dry and liquid ingredients and measuring everything carefully. She asked me at one point how to make the sour milk the recipe called for. "Oh," I said, "put some vinegar or lemon juice in the cup and fill it with milk." Which was she to use, she asked, vinegar or lemon juice? "Oh, it doesn't matter," I replied. She opted for vinegar, then asked how much of it to use. "Oh, about a pour," I told her. At this point, my daughter wisely decided to end all conversation with her mother. The pancakes were very good.

6

Meal #2: This was French toast. The conversation between mother and daughter was considerably shorter than the pancake conversation. When asked about the number of eggs and the quantity of milk required, I replied that it all depended on the number of people being fed, the amount of bread on hand and the size of the eggs you happened to be using. My daughter glared at me and figured it out on her own. The French toast was delicious.

I was not consulted during the making of Meal #3. I was simply called to the table when it was ready. I cleared my own dishes, which redeemed me somewhat in her eyes.

Meal #4: This was perhaps the most trying time my daughter will have this year. The chicken recipe she chose is one that is carried in her mother's head. It involves taking chicken breast, mayonnaise, crushed Ritz crackers, parmesan cheese, salt, pepper and melted butter, putting them all together in a pan and baking them.

"How much mayonnaise?" she asked.

"Some spoonfuls," I replied.

"How many spoonfuls?"

"Oh, just put enough in the bowl. If you run out, take some more."

This she did—but she was not happy about it.

"How many Ritz crackers?" she asked.

"I don't know—a big handful," I replied.

"Your hand or mine?" she asked.

"Whichever," I shrugged. "If you run out, take some more. She glowered at me, but she managed. When it came to cheese and salt and pepper and butter, she was very patient with me while I tried to figure out equivalent measurements for "some," "enough" and "not too much." She was not so patient, though, when it came to cooking time and oven temperature. "You have to cook the chicken at 350 degrees until it's done..." I told her. Her good nature was gone, and it was obvious she was having great difficulty dealing with me. "Fine," she snapped, "but our oven reads 50 degrees warmer than it actually is, so you have to set it at 400. How will I know when it's done?"

"Oh, it should be done about the time you finish mashing the potatoes."

Without ceremony, she kicked me out of the kitchen.

Potato Frittata

All the sleepy eyes in the house will open wide when they know you're serving up a batch of this favorite!

¼ cup olive oil

2 cloves garlic, minced

1 pound frozen shredded hash brown potatoes, thawed

5 eggs

⅓ cup water

½ teaspoon salt

½ teaspoon black pepper

1 tablespoon dried chives

1. In a large nonstick skillet, heat the oil over medium-high heat and sauté the garlic for 10 to 15 seconds. Add the potatoes and continue cooking for about 10 minutes, using a plastic spatula to turn the potatoes occasionally until lightly browned.

2. While the potatoes are cooking, in a medium bowl, whisk together the eggs, water, salt, pepper, and chives. Add the egg mixture to the browned potatoes and reduce the heat to medium. As the mixture begins to set, push it slightly toward the center so that the liquid runs to the edges of the skillet. Reduce the heat to low and cover the skillet. Allow to cook for 11 to 12 minutes.

3. Slide the frittata out of the pan onto a large plate. Invert the skillet over the frittata on the plate and turn the whole frittata over so that the uncooked side is face-down in the skillet. (Be careful, the skillet will be hot.) Cook for 3 to 4 more minutes, until the bottom begins to brown, and serve immediately.

Did You Know . . . *that a frittata is an Italian version of an omelet? Frittatas are firmer than French-style omelets (the traditional type we see more in this country) because they're cooked slowly over low heat, and their ingredients are generally mixed with the eggs and not folded inside.*

Breakfast Burritos

Eggs, meat, vegetables, and bread all rolled into one . . . now that's my idea of a breakfast on the go!

MAKES
10
BURRITOS

1 Preheat the oven to 200°F.

2 Tightly wrap the tortillas in foil and place in the oven for about 15 minutes to warm.

3 Meanwhile, in a large skillet, melt the butter over medium-high heat. Sauté the onion and bell peppers for 6 to 8 minutes, or until tender. Stir in the sausage and sauté for 4 minutes.

4 In a large bowl, combine the eggs, milk, salt, and black pepper; whisk until thoroughly combined. Pour into the skillet over the sausage and vegetables, and cook for 4 to 5 minutes, until the eggs are scrambled and just set. Add the cheese and stir to blend thoroughly.

5 Remove the tortillas from the oven. Place 1/2 cup of the egg mixture down the center of each tortilla, roll up and place seam-side down on a serving platter. Serve immediately.

10 (8-inch) flour tortillas

2 tablespoons butter

1 medium-sized onion, chopped

2 medium-sized green *or* red bell peppers (or 1 of each), chopped

1 package (8 ounces) precooked sausage links, cut into 1/4-inch slices

10 eggs

1/2 cup milk

1/2 teaspoon salt

1/2 teaspoon black pepper

1 1/2 cups (6 ounces) shredded Mexican cheese blend

Timesaving Tip: *Prepare these ahead of time, place the finished burritos in a baking dish, cover with aluminum foil, and keep in a warm oven until ready to serve.*

9

Garden Vegetable Medley

SERVES 4

Looking for something exciting to wake up your family's taste buds? Surprise them with this colorful breakfast treat!

2 tablespoons olive oil

4 cups frozen cubed hash brown potatoes, thawed

2 cups chopped fresh broccoli florets

1 medium-sized red bell pepper, chopped

1 medium-sized onion, chopped

$^3/_4$ teaspoon salt

$^1/_2$ teaspoon black pepper

2 cups sliced fresh mushrooms

8 large eggs, poached

1 In a large skillet, heat the oil over medium-high heat. Add the potatoes, broccoli, bell pepper, onion, salt, and black pepper. Cook for 8 to 10 minutes, or until the potatoes start to brown, stirring occasionally.

2 Add the mushrooms and cook for 4 to 5 minutes, or until tender.

3 Spoon onto plates and top with the poached eggs.

Did You Know . . . *that poached eggs are usually cooked without adding any fat? Here's how to make 'em: In a saucepan, bring 1 to 3 inches of water to a boil. Reduce the heat enough to keep the water simmering gently. Add 1 teaspoon white vinegar. Break an egg into a custard cup or bowl. Holding the dish close to the water's surface, slip the egg into the water; repeat with additional eggs, one at a time. Cook the eggs for 3 to 5 minutes, until the whites are completely set and the yolks begin to thicken, but are not hard. Using a slotted spoon, remove and drain the eggs.*

Never Say "YUCK!"

BY CARYL GINSBURG FANTEL

When Uncle Stan offered me a poached egg covered with mushrooms, I responded a bit too enthusiastically with an emphatic "Yuck!" I don't know why I said it—I liked eggs and I can't recall ever having tried mushrooms before that morning. As soon as the word was out of my mouth, silence descended on our family gathering and everyone at the table stopped filling their brunch plates and stared. What?! What did I do and why was everybody looking at me like that?

"You said, 'Yuck!'" came the loud response to my unspoken questions, "and that means you have to eat it!" Maybe, since I was only five, it hadn't occurred to my dad's lifelong friend, or his family, to share their house rule that if you didn't want any of a particular food that was being served, you were supposed to just say, "No, thank you." If you said "Yuck!" or "No way!" or any other impolite, colorful response you had to eat it.

The memory of that brunch has stuck with me, along with the lessons of not commenting on what other people eat and always being willing to at least try new foods. Those were helpful lessons, especially since we are a "food" family—exposed to lots of interesting foods over the years!

When my brothers and I were growing up, we were the guinea pigs for our parents' catering business menus. When our parents were caterers, before Dad became "Mr. Food," Mom was known for her incredible homemade hors d'oeuvres and other specialties and Dad was known for his beautiful fresh vegetable garnishes and the amazing fruit centerpieces he'd build at their parties. Thanks to those centerpieces, we were introduced to things like kiwifruit in the 1970s (before they were readily available in the U.S.), fresh figs (amazing!), and the most beautiful, huge, long-stemmed strawberries imaginable. Who wouldn't enjoy getting their five daily servings of fruit and vegetables after regular exposure to such variety?

We were expected to try everything. If we didn't like it, that was okay, but at least we had tried it—a philosophy that I think now, as a mother, is not such a bad idea! My daughters, Shayna, 15, and Alyssa, 9, are some of the most adventurous eaters around . . . adults included. Alyssa's best friend's family is from China and they love her visits because she's always game to try their authentic Chinese foods. And last year, Shayna won the unofficial title of "Student Who Brings the Most Interesting Lunches" from her lunch group. One of my proudest "enlightened mommy" moments came when Shayna was in preschool and I had packed dinner leftovers of grilled salmon and asparagus for her lunch one day. Shayna's teachers couldn't get over the fact that this two-year-old was sent to preschool with a lunch like that . . . and had eaten every bit of it! "Kids just don't eat salmon and asparagus!" they said. Our kids do, and I think most will, if that's what they're exposed to early on.

I listen sympathetically to moms complaining that their kids only eat "brown foods" or that they don't like vegetables. I'm sure it's frustrating because that can really limit your family's menus, as well as their nutrition. Introducing different foods—red pepper strips or baby carrots with ranch dressing for a colorful, crunchy, healthy snack; pizza bagels topped with ever-so-tiny pieces of broccoli; and adding things like shredded carrots to spaghetti sauce, or shredded zucchini to meat loaf—usually works to break down that barrier of, "Oh, no, I couldn't eat that!" It's never too late to broaden your children's, or your own, food horizons.

Even though I was "coerced" into trying them when I was five, I didn't actually think that mushrooms were all that bad. Now, I love them. Just ask my girls—I could eat a whole plateful myself at one sitting . . . but I won't, because they want me to share! Thanks, Uncle Stan!

Canadian Breakfast Sandwiches

SERVES 8

No time to prepare for that drop-in company? In just 15 minutes you can be serving a breakfast treat that adults will love . . . and kids, too!

4 English muffins,
  split in half

2 medium tomatoes,
  sliced

8 slices Canadian bacon
  (about 4 ounces total)

8 slices Muenster cheese
  (4 to 5 ounces total)

1 Preheat the broiler. Lay out the English muffins on a cookie sheet and toast them under the broiler for 3 to 5 minutes, or until lightly browned.

2 Layer each muffin half with a slice of tomato, Canadian bacon then cheese. Turn off the broiler and turn on the oven to 350°F.

3 Bake for 7 to 9 minutes, until the cheese is melted and the muffins are heated through.

Did You Know . . . *that Canadian bacon is a leaner alternative to regular bacon? It is actually smoked and cured pork loin and, though it is used pretty much the same way as bacon, Canadian bacon resembles ham in taste and appearance. It can be found in the supermarket along with the regular bacon and pre-sliced meats.*

Slice-'n'-Go Oatmeal

Oatmeal is one of the healthiest foods around, so here's a way to make it into a portable fast food.

MAKES
8 to **10**
SLICES

1. Coat a 9" x 5" loaf pan with nonstick cooking spray.

2. In a large saucepan, bring the water and salt to a boil over high heat. Stir in the oats, and cook for 1 minute. Remove from the heat and stir in the brown sugar and raisins.

3. Pour the oat mixture into the loaf pan, cover, and chill for at least 6 hours, or overnight.

4. Remove loaf from the pan and cut into 1-inch-thick slices.

5. In a large skillet, melt 1 tablespoon butter over medium heat. Cook the oatmeal slices for 2 to 3 minutes per side, or until golden and heated through, adding more butter as necessary. Optional reheating method: Microwave slices for 1 to 2 minutes, until warmed through.

6 cups water

1 teaspoon salt

3½ cups quick-cooking oats

½ cup brown sugar

1 cup raisins

3 tablespoons butter, divided (optional, see Step 5)

Serving Tip: *Serve slices topped with additional brown sugar or warm maple syrup.*

Timesaving Tip: *This is a terrific make-ahead dish, 'cause all you have to do is warm it and take it with you. Along with a banana or some fresh berries, it makes a quick and complete breakfast.*

Fruity Pancake Muffins

MAKES 1 dozen MUFFINS

Mmm, there's nothing like one of those big old-fashioned breakfasts that Mom used to make. But honestly, today we know that there's a better way to go than loading up on all the bacon, sausage, ham, potatoes, and pancakes that used to be a part of it, so here's a breakfast recipe you're gonna love.

2 cups packaged pancake and waffle mix

2 eggs

1 cup milk

$\frac{1}{2}$ cup club soda

1 tablespoon vegetable oil

1 cup fresh blueberries *or* peeled and chopped apples

$\frac{1}{4}$ cup pancake syrup

1 Preheat the oven to 350°F. Coat a 12-cup muffin tin with nonstick cooking spray.

2 In a large bowl, combine the pancake mix, eggs, milk, club soda, and oil; mix well. Pour evenly into the muffin cups and sprinkle with the fruit.

3 Bake for 20 to 25 minutes, or until a wooden toothpick inserted in the center comes out clean. Remove from the oven and brush the tops with pancake syrup. Serve warm.

Option: *If you're craving that old-fashioned breakfast combo, you can substitute 4 chopped heat-and-serve beef sausages (half of a 5.2-ounce package) for the fruit in here.*

Baked Apple Pancake

You ask the gang what they want for breakfast and they say pancakes. They're not hard to make, but by the time you finish all the batches and you finally get to sit down, everybody else is practically done. No more! With this recipe, you make one big pancake and cut it into pieces. It tastes the same and now every-body gets to eat together. I think that's the best "OOH IT'S SO GOOD!!®"

SERVES
9 to 12

1 Preheat the oven to 425°F. Coat a 10" x 15" rimmed baking sheet with nonstick cooking spray.

2 In a large bowl, combine all the ingredients except the apples; beat well with a whisk. Stir the apples into the batter and pour onto the baking sheet.

3 Bake for 12 to 14 minutes, or until the pancake is lightly browned on top. Cut into serving-sized pieces.

2¼ cups packaged pancake and waffle mix

1½ cups milk

2 eggs

3 tablespoons sugar

1 tablespoon vegetable oil

1 teaspoon ground cinnamon

1½ cups cored, peeled, and chopped apples (about 2 small apples)

Serving Tip: *Top these with butter and maple syrup. And if you want, go ahead and add fresh blueberries to the batter for even richer fruit flavor!*

Every Mom Is a
WORKING MOM

BY ANN MORROW

For years I loved being a stay-at-home mom. I enjoyed the full-time responsibility of taking care of my home and family. But once all the kids were in school and my days became void of a young child's needs, I felt the need to return to the workforce and contribute to our family's financial well-being. Mostly, I wanted to preserve the little sanity I had left. I had to get out of the house before I went bonkers.

The job search itself can be a little more than intimidating. I'm not one of those women who returned to the work force when the baby was six weeks old. After years of following four kids around with a damp cloth and a dustpan, being a full-time mom was my work force. While career women were out changing the world, I was changing diapers. When the first American woman was climbing Mt. Everest, I was scaling a mound of dirty laundry. And when Shirley Muldowney was setting speed records, I was racing through the house after a muddy dog and three giggling toddlers. Who had time for a career? I was busy being a mommy and working toward a goal of being the first woman alive who could make a four-year-old eat Brussels sprouts without gagging.

I sat down with a variety of job applications strewn before me. I managed to complete the Name and Address part without any problem, but when I got to the questions, I froze. Position Desired? I ambitiously wrote, "I'll take what I can get." Next question. Pay Expected? My pen hit the page before I had a chance to think, and I answered with, "At least $1 an hour more than my babysitter gets." By the time I reached the bottom of the application, I started getting frustrated, and I flung my pen across the table when I read, Indicate All Positions Held over the Past Five Years. Well that was easy—or would have been easy—if I had in fact received any money for the following:

Short Order Cook: Responsibilities include creating last-minute meals from nothing more than leftover macaroni and three stalks of celery. Preparing snacks for entire Little League teams with no advance notice and dealing with troublesome customers who insist on consuming nothing less than a sandwich that looks like something from a cookbook page.

Gourmet Chef: Entails same job duties as above, only with a better class of leftovers.

Bookkeeper/Accountant: Thirteen years of experience balancing a messy checkbook, doling out allowances, purchasing groceries for a family of six—on a budget for a family of three—and somehow making a house payment at Christmas time.

Maid/Janitor: Four kids, plus multiple pets—you do the math.

Chauffeur: Have driven approximately 182,450 miles delivering children to school, dental appointments, birthday parties, Grandma's house and sporting events.

Door-to-Door Salesman: Nine years of experience in product solicitation, from Girl Scout cookies to raffle tickets for the school band.

The last thing left for me to complete was a section that required listing any special skills that would make me a candidate for the job. I thought about it, then wrote: "I possess great people skills with the ability to delegate fairly, yet with authority. Can deal with difficult individuals and am capable of resolving disputes. Able to work varying hours and have been known to work twenty-four-hour shifts when needed. Accustomed to working in undesirable conditions with little or no gratitude. Strong verbal communication skills and willingness to perform managerial duties." All of which translates to, "I've been managing a family budget, bossing the kids around and breaking up fights for the past thirteen years, and no one has ever thanked me for it. Do I get the job?"

I can also braid hair, remove gum from shag carpet, untie knots from muddy shoelaces, bathe a cat, change a tire and have an unusually high tolerance for boogery noses. With a list of qualifications like that, how can any employer pass me up?

3-2-1 Power Bars

Everybody can use an extra boost in the morning, especially on Mondays! Go ahead and try a 3–2–1 power bar . . . but be prepared to blast into the busy week ahead.

3 cups granola with fruit and nuts (see Hint)

2 cups crispy rice cereal

1 cup sweetened dried cranberries

3 tablespoons butter

24 marshmallows

Healthy Hint:

To give these the most flavor, choose a granola that has lots of fruit and nuts.

1. Coat a 9" x 13" baking dish with nonstick cooking spray.

2. In a large bowl, combine the granola, cereal, and cranberries; mix well. Melt the butter in a soup pot over low heat. Add the marshmallows and, stirring constantly, cook until melted and smooth.

3. Remove from the heat and stir in the granola mixture until well combined. Spoon the mixture into the baking dish and pat down evenly.

4. Let sit for 15 minutes, or until firm, then cut into bars. Serve, or store in an airtight container until ready to serve.

Timesaving Tip: *This is a perfect make-ahead breakfast item to have on hand for those mornings when you and the family have to "grab and go."*

Breakfast Cookies

Instead of serving individual breakfast shakes and granola, why not combine them in the form of a tasty cookie?

MAKES
about **3**
DOZEN

1 Preheat the oven to 350°F.

2 Place 1½ cups cereal in a shallow dish, breaking up the larger pieces; set aside.

3 In a large bowl, cream the butter, brown sugar, instant breakfast mix, and egg until smooth. Add the flour, baking powder, and cinnamon; beat until thoroughly combined. Add the remaining 3 cups cereal; beat until well mixed.

4 Form into 1-inch balls and coat in the reserved cereal, rolling to coat completely. Place on cookie sheets 2 inches apart.

5 Bake for 12 to 14 minutes, or until firm and light golden. Serve warm, or allow to cool and store in an airtight container.

4½ cups granola cereal with raisins, divided

½ cup (1 stick) butter, softened

½ cup packed light brown sugar

1 envelope (1¼ ounces) vanilla instant breakfast drink mix

1 egg

¾ cup all-purpose flour

¼ teaspoon baking powder

½ teaspoon ground cinnamon

Option: *It's easy to change the flavor of the cookies simply by using a different-flavored breakfast drink mix.*

21

Strawberry-Banana Smoothie

SERVES 4

What a perfect way to get the kids—and you—started in the morning! A glassful of this has lots of goodness.

2 packages
(10 ounces each)
frozen sliced straw-
berries in syrup

2 containers
(8 ounces each)
strawberry yogurt

1 ripe banana, peeled

1 cup milk

1 In a blender, blend all the ingredients for 1 to 2 minutes, or until smooth and creamy.

2 Pour into glasses and serve immediately.

Option: *For that taste of summer, you can't beat a smoothie made with frozen peach slices and peach yogurt, but almost any frozen fruit and matching flavor yogurt can be made into your special fruit smoothie.*

Did You Know . . . *that the latest government studies say we all need a minimum of five servings a day of fruit and vegetables? This is a great way to get your family started off right.*

SUPER MOM

BY JAYE LEWIS

My greatest ambition, as a young mother, was to become a Super Mom. You know Super Mom! Her hair never droops, is limp or flies away. It's always perfect, either straight, but stylishly swinging to her shoulders, or softly curled, with a slightly wind-blown effect. Her figure is slim, and her clothes always hang just so.

Super Mom never throws anything out. I've been told, on good authority, that she doesn't even have garbage. Empty cans become lovely pencil holders with the help of a little glue and a few scraps of material. Vegetable peelings become miniature compost, and, of course, the tops of carrots and the pits of avocados (due to her perpetual green thumb) soon become lovely plants to be given away to all her friends.

Super Mom never sweats. She doesn't even perspire. She just glows. Her dishes are always done. At dinner time, you can walk into her kitchen, unannounced, as she's making meat loaf, baking a fresh apple pie and squeezing fresh juice for dinner. Nothing is out of place. Ingredients appear and disappear like magic, leaving no tell-tale signs of peelings, sugar, spices or globs of flour. In an instant, meat loaf is done to perfection; the pie is bubbling in the oven; and dishes and pans have disappeared without a trace.

Super Mom's children never run in and out to distract her. She never has to patch a piecrust that has been lovingly destroyed by an overzealous, smiling four-year-old. Without any assistance from eager, little hands, she is absolutely perfect.

My children lived in my kitchen, with three sets of hands squeezing the meat loaf, peeling apples, and dusting the counter with spices and crumbs. The floor was always littered with trails of bread crumbs and apple peelings, while much care had to be taken to keep from sliding across the floor.

One day, I thought I had arrived at Super Mom status. I had awakened early, zipped through housework, baked a loaf of bread, coordinated my clothes with my shoes and purse, had patience with the children, and arrived on time at a club meeting for the local Super Moms. I was glowing, instead of sweating; my coif was perfect; my clothes were tasteful; and my nails . . . my nails! I spent the next hour and a half trying to pick out all the dried bread dough from underneath my fingernails!

Oh, woe is me! I never fully arrived at Super Mom status, and I thank God for that. I would have had to give up so many wonderful things—sweaty hugs, peanut-butter kisses and brushing away tears from a dirty upturned face. Most of all, I would have missed that blissful treasure of a small pair of arms slipping around my neck as I plumped pillows and smoothed covers. I would never have heard those tender, precious words: "Mommy, I love you!" I wouldn't have had time to drop to my knees and thank God for his great blessing in making me a mother. So, who wants to be a Super Mom? Not me! I'm still working on just plain Mommy!

Frozen Banana Latte

Bananas and chocolate are a heavenly combination that we can enjoy in the morning without any guilt when we combine them in this yummy breakfast drink!

1½ cups strong cold
black coffee

¾ cup half-and-half

2 frozen bananas,
cut in half (see Tip)

2 tablespoons chocolate
flavor syrup

¼ cup sugar

½ cup ice cubes

1 In a blender jar, combine all the ingredients and blend until frothy.

2 Pour into glasses and serve immediately.

Money-Saving Tip: *Bananas too ripe to eat? No need to throw them out! Just freeze them to use in this recipe, a fruit smoothie, or for banana bread.*

Healthy Hint:

Substitute decaf for regular coffee, milk for the half-and-half, use low-fat chocolate flavor syrup, and sugar substitute for the sugar.

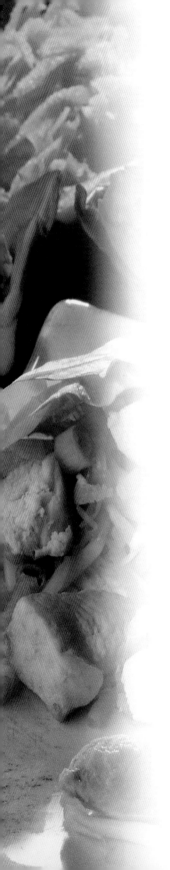

Fast Chicken Fajitas

When we order these in a restaurant, usually when we get past the steam and the sizzle we're left with a small portion of chicken and a high price tag! So, why not bring the sizzle to your own kitchen table with a dish that's sure to satisfy your tummy and your wallet?

MAKES
10
FAJITAS

1 In a large skillet, heat the oil over medium-high heat. Add the onions and peppers and sauté for 3 to 5 minutes, or until the onions are tender, stirring occasionally.

2 In a small bowl, combine the chicken and the fajita seasoning until the chicken is thoroughly coated. Add to the skillet and cook for 5 to 6 minutes, or until no pink remains in the chicken and the onions are browned, stirring frequently.

3 Distribute the chicken mixture evenly over the tortillas. Top with the salsa and lettuce then roll up the tortillas and serve immediately.

1 tablespoon vegetable oil

2 large onions, cut into 8 wedges each

1 large green bell pepper, cut into $1/2$-inch strips

1 large red bell pepper, cut into $1/2$-inch strips

1 pound boneless, skinless chicken breast, cut into $1/2$-inch strips

2 tablespoons dry fajita seasoning

10 (8-inch) flour tortillas

1 cup salsa

$1/2$ of a medium head iceberg lettuce, shredded (about 4 cups)

Healthy Hint:

To make these even more nutritious, use whole-wheat tortillas.

29

Asian Wraps

For your next party, why not serve up some fun by putting out this chicken mixture with Bibb lettuce leaves and letting everybody fold their own wraps?! Not only is this a timesaver for you, but it lets your family and guests in on the action, too.

2 cups cooked chicken breast chunks

¼ pound fresh bean sprouts

½ small head Napa *or* Chinese cabbage, shredded (about 3 cups)

1 medium carrot, shredded (about 1 cup)

6 scallions, thinly sliced

¼ cup white vinegar

3 tablespoons canola oil

2 tablespoons light soy sauce

1 tablespoon sesame oil

2 garlic cloves, minced

2 teaspoons ground ginger

½ teaspoon black pepper

1 to 2 heads Bibb lettuce, separated to obtain 16 leaves

1 In a large bowl, combine the chicken, bean sprouts, cabbage, carrot, and scallions; mix well.

2 In a small bowl, combine the vinegar, canola oil, soy sauce, sesame oil, garlic, ginger, and black pepper; mix well then pour over the cabbage mixture. Mix until evenly coated.

3 Spoon an equal amount of the chicken mixture onto the center of each lettuce leaf and fold like an envelope. Place wraps seam-side down on a serving platter and serve immediately.

Leftover Tip: *This dish is so much fun to make that when you cook chicken breasts for other dishes, you're gonna want to make extra just so you'll have some left over to make this! You can also use the leftovers from your rotisserie chicken.*

Option: *You can replace the dressing ingredients in Step 2 with ⅔ cup of your favorite Asian dressing.*

Thinking Outside the Box Lunch

BY JEAN BLACKMER

It was the first day of school and the first time my friend would be sending all three of her children off for a full day. She sat down at the kitchen table, put her elbows on it, and rested her head on her hands. Then, silently, the tears began to flow down her cheeks. She didn't notice her youngest son standing in the doorway watching her.

After a few moments, he walked over to her and put his hand on her shoulder. "It's okay, Mommy. I'll be back after school."

"Oh, hi, sweetie," she said as she turned and gave him a hug. "I know, but I'll miss you so much." She told me she didn't have the heart to tell him that she wasn't crying because he, her third and final child, was off to school. The truth was she was crying because she now had to make three lunches every day.

"I know the feeling," I said after laughing with her.

My three boys refuse to eat the school hot lunches. They complain about the rubbery chicken nuggets and the tater tots that bounce on the floor.

For me, making lunches fits into the same dull category as folding laundry, grocery shopping, vacuuming and even cleaning the bathrooms.

Our mornings are already so chaotic. Getting three boys off to school clean, dressed, fed and with a healthy sack lunch often puts me over the edge. Our kitchen counters are usually covered with debris from breakfast—spilled milk, sticky honey, bread crumbs, dirty cups, banana peels, spoons and bowls. Add to that the mustard stains, cheese scraps, broken potato chips and cookie crumbs, and I end up hollering at everyone to do a quick kitchen cleanup before we're ready to head out the door.

I can't even count the number of days when I've gotten into the car, driven the boys to school, then realized I was still wearing my slippers, or only put on one earring, or only managed to apply mascara to one of my eyes. It's overwhelming and embarrassing to say the least.

Once, when I was exasperated from our stress-filled morning routine, an older, wiser woman reminded me that in life we have a choice. We can either choose to become bitter, or we can become better. I started to see myself becoming bitter about all I had to do in the morning. How I hated to wake up to such chaos and rushing around.

I knew I needed an attitude adjustment. I started by playing upbeat music in the morning. Music is known to decrease stress (at least that's what one article I read said), and our mornings were chock-full of stress.

I also started asking my friends what they made their kids for lunch. One mom said she tries to buy different kinds of breads to add a little variety to the monotonous sandwich, like croissants, bagels or rolls. This tip motivated me to try and think "outside of the box lunch." I started buying frozen French bread pizzas for the older boys to cook in their schools' microwaves. I made pot stickers, wraps with tortillas, and bought a small thermos for noodles and soups.

Making lunches became a challenge. The boys even got caught up in the game and began coming up with creative ideas for their lunches. They'll stick in granola and yogurt, use leftover sausage links for sandwiches with spaghetti sauce for dipping, and have occasionally convinced me to buy pre-made sushi from the grocery store. Some mornings I still end up hollering, over the music, for everyone to help me clean up. Sometimes during the mad rush out the door I still forget to take off my slippers. And some mornings making three sack lunches just doesn't happen. Then, I tell myself it's okay. I hand the boys a healthy granola bar and a few dollars for the school hot lunch. When they moan, I remind them to be grateful for the food we do have and to remember they have a choice. They can become bitter or better—even if it means better at bouncing those little tater tots into the trashcan where they belong.

Farmer's Chicken Fingers

SERVES 4 to 5

I guarantee you've never had chicken fingers quite like these. The tiny fingers at your table are gonna be picking them up as fast as you can serve 'em!

1 bag (6 ounces) potato chips, crushed

½ cup ranch salad dressing

1 pound boneless, skinless chicken breast, cut into ½-inch strips

Healthy Hint:

To make these lighter, use light ranch dressing and baked potato chips instead of standard fried chips.

1 Preheat the oven to 400°F. Coat a baking sheet with nonstick cooking spray.

2 Place the crushed potato chips in a shallow bowl; place the dressing in another shallow bowl.

3 Dip the chicken into the dressing, coating completely and shaking off any excess dressing. Coat the chicken with the crushed potato chips then place on the baking sheet.

4 Bake for 15 to 18 minutes, or until the chicken is cooked through.

Serving Tip: *Kids love to dip! My grandchildren like dipping these in ketchup. And we give 'em carrot sticks to dip in ranch salad dressing as a great go-along.*

Champion Chili

Everybody's got a favorite chili recipe, and this one's mine, because it not only tastes great, but we don't need to do much to it except stir; the cooktop does most of the work.

SERVES 8 to 10

1. In a soup pot, brown the ground beef, sausage, onions, and garlic over high heat for 20 to 25 minutes, stirring frequently.

2. Add the remaining ingredients; mix well and bring to a boil. Reduce the heat to medium-low and simmer for 30 minutes, stirring occasionally.

Serving Tip: *Top with all your favorite chili toppings from shredded cheese to chopped onions and sliced jalapeño peppers.*

Timesaving Tip: *This is a perfect recipe to keep on hand in the slow cooker on those after-noons or evenings when everybody's coming home and eating at different times.*

2½ pounds lean ground beef

1½ pounds Italian sausage, casing removed

2 large onions, chopped

2 garlic cloves, minced

2 cans (15½ ounces each) dark red kidney beans, undrained

1 can (28 ounces) crushed tomatoes

¼ cup chili powder

1 teaspoon ground cumin

1 teaspoon salt

½ teaspoon black pepper

Veggie-Packed Pizza

SERVES 4 to 6

Even though your neighborhood pizzeria might make a tasty cheese pizza, why not save some dough and use your own dough for this homemade pizza packed with fresh veggies?

1 (12-inch) prepared pizza shell

1 cup pizza or spaghetti sauce

1 can (2¼ ounces) sliced black olives, drained

1 jar (2½ ounces) sliced mushrooms, drained

1 jar (7 ounces) roasted red peppers, drained and cut into thin strips

1 cup (4 ounces) shredded mozzarella cheese

1 container (2.8 ounces) French-fried onions

1 Preheat the oven to 375°F.

2 Place the pizza shell on a pizza pan. Spread with the pizza sauce and top evenly with the black olives, mushrooms, and roasted peppers. Sprinkle with the cheese and French-fried onions.

3 Bake for 15 to 18 minutes, or until the cheese is melted and the crust is crisp and golden. Slice and serve.

Healthy Hint:

To make this even more nutritious, use light pizza sauce, part-skim mozzarella cheese, and substitute thinly sliced fresh onions for the French-fried onions.

Homestyle Macaroni and Cheese

Moms of yesterday and today have one big thing in common: how much you care about what your families eat. By pairing this crowd-pleasing main dish (loaded with all-important calcium) with some steamed veggies and a salad, you'll be sure to satisfy everybody.

SERVES
6

1 Preheat the oven to 375°F. Coat a 9" x 13" baking dish with nonstick cooking spray.

2 Cook the macaroni according to the package directions; drain. Place half in the bottom of the baking dish.

3 In a medium saucepan, melt the butter over medium heat. Add the flour, salt, and pepper; stir to mix well. Gradually add the milk; bring to a boil and cook until thickened, stirring constantly. Sprinkle 1½ cups cheese over the macaroni in the baking dish and top with half of the white sauce. Repeat the layers once more then top with the remaining 1 cup cheese.

4 Bake for 35 to 40 minutes, or until heated through and the top is golden. Serve immediately.

1 pound elbow macaroni

¼ cup (½ stick) butter

2 tablespoons all-purpose flour

1 teaspoon salt

½ teaspoon black pepper

2 cups milk

4 cups (16 ounces) shredded sharp Cheddar cheese

Healthy Hint:

This is sure to create smiles when you pack it in your kids' lunch thermoses. If they have it along with a cup of low-fat milk, they'll be well on their way to getting their daily calcium requirements.

IN THE BAG

BY DEBBIE FARMER

Every day I try to send my daughter to school with a homemade lunch just like my mother used to make. I put it in a colorful bag along with a special message that she can read while she eats.

Unfortunately, my high expectations slowly descend into the abyss of reality during the course of the week, and my daughter can tell what day it is by the content of her lunch bag.

On Monday, I am perky and bright-eyed. I snap open her lunch bag and ponder the four food groups. I lovingly prepare a bunch of juicy grapes, two different kinds of homemade cookies, a container of soup, a bottle of fresh squeezed orange juice, and a sandwich (which I trim into fun little shapes with cookie cutters).

I contemplate her note: "Darling princess, you are the light of my life. Do your best work at school. I will see you when you get home. Lots of love, Mom." I can barely find enough room in the bag to slide it in.

On Tuesday, I am a little less perky. I set her bag on the counter and try to recycle what is left over from Monday. I add more water to the soup and stuff the remaining pieces of homemade cookies into a baggie. We're running late, so I substitute the grapes with a box of raisins. I barely have time to cut her sandwich in half before closing the bag. I quickly add a note: "Do your best as you always do. I am proud of you. Love, Mom."

By Wednesday, some of the food is already gone so I have to substitute. "Where's my fruit?" My daughter looks into her bag, which I threw on the counter.

"It's in the jelly in your sandwich."

"Oh. Can I have some cheese, too?"

"Sure." I rip open a box of macaroni and cheese, grab a package of cheddar flavoring, and quickly toss it into the bag. Then I scrawl: "Princess, do good today. See you soon. Love, Mom."

By Thursday, I am definitely no longer bright-eyed or perky, and I begin to think it's okay to make a sandwich out of two peanut butter and granola bars because it will cover most of the major food groups and I am out of bread. Instead I roll a slice of bologna into a tortilla and toss a lemon into the bag for vitamin C. Then I add a box of Cracker Jacks since popcorn is a vegetable. I grab a piece of paper and quickly write: "Have a great day. Love, Mom. P.S. If the lunchroom monitor sees your lunch, don't give her your real name."

By Friday, I invent a fifth food group usually called "The Mystery Meat Group," and I scrawl a message on the back of my daughter's lunch bag that reads: "To whom it may concern, please believe I am really a good mother." I begin to feel guilty and wonder if other better-organized mothers sent wonderful culinary creations for their children every day. Maybe sending a homemade lunch to school for my daughter isn't the right thing for me to do.

"Do you want to buy lunch instead?" I ask as I hand her the lunch bag.

"No way! Friday's my favorite lunch day!"

I stare at her blankly.

"I can trade my granola bar for Jimmy's leftover Thursday night pizza. Then, if I add a bag of graham crackers and a box of raisins, I can trade up for Meg's tuna and ketchup sandwich. If I throw in two lemons, I'll have enough for Susie's turkey and mustard salad on a bagel and a bag of chocolate-chip cookies."

As I watch her walk down the driveway happily swinging her lunch bag, I remember some of the lunch room deals I made as a child. Then I realize that even though I'm a failure at making lunches like my mother, I'm a success at passing on the art of lunch-bag substitution.

Deli Wraps

When it comes to portable lunches, the wraps have it! (And these are so fresh and colorful, the kids'll never trade 'em for something else!)

¼ cup light mayonnaise

4 (10-inch) flour tortillas

¾ pound sliced deli ham

1 package (8 ounces) fresh baby spinach

¾ pound sliced deli turkey

16 slices (12 ounces total) yellow American cheese

1 Spread equal amounts of mayonnaise on each tortilla. Layer each tortilla with equal amounts of ham, spinach, turkey, and cheese.

2 Roll up each tortilla jelly-roll-style and place each one seam-side down on a separate piece of waxed paper. Roll up in the waxed paper, tying each end. Slice in half, and serve.

Option: Keep 'em guessing and use a different flavor or type of tortilla, such as spinach, sun-dried tomato, or even whole-wheat, each time you make these.

Baked Italian Heros

MAKES
6
SANDWICHES

This is no ordinary sandwich—it's a combination of hearty meats, cheese, and veggies layered and baked to perfection. Give it a try!

6 (6- to 8-inch) hero (hoagie) rolls, split

½ cup Italian dressing

½ pound sliced deli salami

½ pound sliced deli turkey

½ pound sliced deli ham

½ pound sliced deli provolone cheese

1 large tomato, thinly sliced

½ of a medium onion, thinly sliced

1 Preheat the oven to 375°F. Brush the cut sides of the rolls with the Italian dressing.

2 Layer the bottom halves of the rolls with the salami, turkey, ham, cheese, tomato, and onion; replace the tops of the rolls. Place each sandwich on a piece of aluminum foil and wrap tightly.

3 Bake for 12 to 15 minutes, or until the cheese is melted. Carefully remove the aluminum foil and serve.

Option: *Depending on where you're from, you may call a hero sandwich a submarine, grinder, hoagie or poor boy (known as a "po'boy" in New Orleans). It's fun to layer your choice of meats, veggies, cheese, and condiments on a French bread, Italian bread or hoagie roll, so use these, or create your own different combination every time!*

Croissant Club

Let's try something different! When we make a club sandwich, instead of frying bacon, try using a shortcut with bacon mayonnaise. It's a true timesaver—and isn't that what sandwiches are all about?

MAKES
8
SANDWICHES

1. In a small bowl, combine the mayonnaise and bacon bits; mix well and spread equally over the croissant halves.

2. Layer the lettuce, tomato, and turkey equally over the bottom croissant halves; replace the tops of the croissants and serve.

1 cup mayonnaise

2 tablespoons real bacon bits

8 large croissants, split

8 romaine lettuce leaves

1 large tomato, cut into 8 slices (see Tip)

1 pound thinly sliced deli turkey

Option: It's a nice change of pace to use things like croissants for our sandwiches. Don't forget to try other non-traditional breads like tortillas for making sandwich wraps, pitas for making stuffed sandwiches, and English muffins for making toasted sandwiches.

Preparation Tip: Cut each slice of tomato in half so the slices will fit on the croissants.

43

Fresh Veggie Pita

MAKES 6 SANDWICHES

Fresh and simple, this garden veggie pocket is versatile enough for all year 'round. Enjoy it with a bowl of soup for a light dinner, or pack it in the lunch boxes on days when you're on the go . . . and when you're watching your waistline!

2 large cucumbers, peeled, seeded, and finely chopped

1 container (16 ounces) plain yogurt

1 tablespoon sugar

1 teaspoon garlic powder

$1/8$ teaspoon salt

$1/8$ teaspoon black pepper

$1/2$ of a medium-sized head iceberg lettuce, coarsely chopped

1 package (6 ounces) alfalfa sprouts

1 large tomato, seeded and chopped

1 medium-sized carrot, grated

1 medium-sized red bell pepper, diced

$1/2$ of a small onion, diced

6 whole-wheat or regular pita breads, cut in half

1. In a medium bowl, combine the cucumbers, yogurt, sugar, garlic powder, salt, and black pepper; mix well.

2. In a large bowl, combine the remaining ingredients except the pita bread; mix well. Stuff the pita halves equally with the lettuce mixture then top with the cucumber sauce, and serve.

Did You Know . . . that pita bread is Middle Eastern flat bread? Now available in most U.S. supermarkets, pita bread has become very popular here. Pita rounds can be split horizontally to form a pocket for all types of sandwich ingredients, or cut into wedges for use as dippers. Try 'em for the Garlic Pita Crisps and Roasted Red Pepper Hummus recipes (pages 68 and 60).

IF YOU BUILD IT, They Will Come!

BY M. MYLENE ENGLISH

It's not a bad deal, really, a quarter for some citrus juice and a smile. You'll probably get a story to go with it (they're good at telling stories, these three), and they'll wish you a nice day as you leave. They set it up on the front lawn. Two of my children do the work, and a third looks on, making suggestions and offering to sample the product. There is now a lemonade stand on my lawn. Twenty-five cents a glass.

I watch them sitting on little white chairs behind their little white table, waiting for their first customer. They firmly believe that "if you build it, they will come," and I firmly believe in their faith. Looking at the drizzle-gray sky, how could I do anything but support their endeavor? They are out there, huddled in their jackets, turning in their chairs to put their backs to the wind. Waiting. Expectant. Hopeful.

I could explain to them that their business would stand a greater chance of success on a hot Saturday afternoon. I could tell them about location and advertising and promotion and timing, about filling a need and creating desire. I could tell them all I know of the adult business world, but it would serve no purpose. They want to do this. They have determination. They have the energy and the resources . . . me. They have tapped me for juice, glasses, jugs, hot water and soap. I have "loaned" them money for their float, and we have practiced making change. I have done all I can. The rest is up to them.

My brother and I sold lemonade at such a stand when we were their age. We planned and prepared. We waited and hoped. We knew nothing of profit and loss, and we really didn't care. We sold one glass of lemonade; we made a nickel; we were happy. Watching now, I know how it is with my children. They have given four glasses of juice for free to friends. (First rule of business: Don't give away the farm.)

But while they weren't looking, someone left four quarters on their table. Someone who was once their age, who, not so long ago, sold lemonade by the glass at a stand on the very same front lawn, poured from the very same pitcher. Someone who also believes in the power of hope and the love of an older sister. It's not a bad deal, really, two bits for some citrus juice and a smile. Wanna buy a dream?

Ham and Nacho Cheese Roll-Ups

SERVES 4

Olé! This south-of-the-border lunch is a tasty alternative to that old standby, PB&J.

4 (6- or 8-inch) flour tortillas

½ cup nacho cheese spread

1 cup crushed tortilla chips

4 slices (4 ounces total) deli ham

1 Place the tortillas on a flat surface and spread evenly with the cheese spread.

2 Sprinkle each with the crushed tortilla chips and top with a slice of ham. Roll up tightly jelly-roll-style and wrap each in waxed paper or plastic wrap. Chill until ready to serve.

Preparation Tip: *The perfect make-ahead lunchbox meal, these roll-ups are actually better when chilled overnight—it helps them hold together better. Serve whole or sliced to look like colorful pinwheels.*

Healthy Hint:

Use whole-wheat tortillas to make these even more nutritious.

46

BLT Burritos

No need to drive through a Mexican fast-food place, 'cause we can have a home-made fiesta anytime . . . right at home! Fold up these quick-and-easy burritos and enjoy!

MAKES 4 BURRITOS

1. In a large bowl, combine the lettuce, tomato, mayonnaise, bacon bits, and pepper; mix well.

2. Spoon the mixture evenly onto the centers of the tortillas. Fold up the bottom of each tortilla over the lettuce mixture then fold both sides over, envelope fashion. Fold the top of each tortilla closed and turn seam-side down. Serve immediately.

6 cups shredded iceberg lettuce

1 medium ripe tomato, chopped

1 cup mayonnaise

1 container (3 ounces) real bacon bits (see Hint)

1/8 teaspoon black pepper

4 (10-inch) flour tortillas

Healthy Hint:

If you'd prefer, use light mayonnaise and whole-wheat tortillas and, instead of bacon bits, chop a quarter pound of deli turkey to mix in and create a "TLT" burrito.

47

Mexican Tortilla Soup

SERVES 6 to 8

This hearty soup not only tastes terrific but looks great too! Check it out on the facing page.

1 tablespoon vegetable oil

1 pound boneless, skinless chicken breasts, cut into ½-inch chunks

1 red bell pepper, coarsely chopped

3 garlic cloves, minced

3 cans (14 ounces each) ready-to-serve reduced-sodium chicken broth

1 package (10 ounces) frozen whole kernel corn

½ cup salsa

¼ cup chopped fresh cilantro

1 cup broken-up baked tortilla chips

1 In a soup pot, heat the oil over medium heat. Add the chicken, bell pepper, and garlic, and cook for about 3 minutes, or until the chicken is browned, stirring frequently.

2 Stir in the chicken broth, corn, and salsa; bring to a boil. Reduce the heat to low, cover, and simmer for 5 minutes, or until no pink remains in the chicken.

3 Stir in the cilantro, ladle into bowls, and serve topped with the tortilla chips.

OPTION: *If you have it on hand, you can use the kernels from two to three ears of fresh corn in place of canned here.*

Did You Know . . . *that we have lots of choices when it comes to finding healthier alternatives to the regular products we have in our pantries? One easy choice is baked tortilla chips.*

Tortilla Soup Torment

BY ROBIN EHRLICHMAN WOODS

My children look forward to the changing seasons with glee. Colder temperatures kick off my soup-making season, especially my delicious Tortilla Soup. It's an easy, tasty and spicy soup that warms the cockles of your heart. I make a huge pot of it, and we can feast on it for days. All it needs as an accompaniment are some nacho chips, and we're good to go.

My daughter and son participate in this rare occurrence: a meal made with fresh ingredients, with lots of chopping and dicing action. I want them to know that I can cook more than reheated fish sticks and chicken nuggets. My son still believes that I invented his all-time favorite: English muffin pizzas.

The last time that I prepared the soup, however, I inadvertently set my offsprings' bellies on fire. It was innocent enough, or so I thought. My children still hold a grudge against me, choosing to believe that the fiery results were premeditated.

We took a short trip to the store for the ingredients. All I needed was canned chicken broth, garlic, salsa, onions, cilantro and a jalapeño pepper. The combination of the sautéed ingredients and the rich chicken broth make for a fine main course or appetizer.

In the produce section, I picked up a beautiful bunch of cilantro, which I love to cook with. It seems to brighten up everything, although I must resist the urge to bake with it. Usually, I pick out a small jalapeño pepper to chop up and simmer in the soup, but my eyes were drawn to a colorful basket of tiny peppers. Examining them closer, they looked like adorable cherry tomatoes, but they were red, yellow and green. We purchased them to add to the soup, deciding that they would not only add flavor, but visual appeal as well. How brilliant of me to combine cooking and art in one project.

I unearthed my large soup kettle hidden by pots, pans and skillets, and began to assemble the ingredients. In just a few minutes, the kitchen was redolent with smells of garlic and onions. The kids dropped in bits and pieces of cilantro, expertly torn by hand. The adorable little peppers cooked happily and looked very colorful simmering in the broth.

After the soup simmered for fifteen minutes, I taste-tested it to see if it needed more salt. Wow! It had a little bite to it, which I found helpful in clearing my sinuses and warming my stomach. I ladled portions into large colorful bowls and called everyone to the table. Topping each portion with nacho chips and crunchy tortilla strips, I waited for the "oohs" and "aahs" of appreciation.

My son took his first slurp of soup.

In seconds, he pushed the bowl away from him, turned lobster-red and jumped up from his seat. What was wrong?

Well . . . the soup not only had a little bite to it, but also was extraordinarily spicy. I tasted the soup again and began to cough discreetly into a napkin. Gee whiz, who turned up the heat? My daughter sipped away happily, although she drank copious amounts of water after each spoonful, tears running down her cheeks.

Unbeknownst to me, I had purchased incredibly hot habanera peppers. The package of peppers had not been marked with a skull and crossbones, and I assumed that such tiny, cute things could only add flavor and pizzazz to my soup. I was very hurt that anyone would think that I knowingly tried to harm them with my cooking.

The next day, I went back to the produce department to speak to one of the employees. I was wondering what all the fuss was about with those darn peppers. When he informed me that I had purchased murderous habaneras, I was aghast. How could those colorful, sweet things be so dangerous? He laughed when I told him about my family's reaction, suggesting that I invest in a new can opener instead of a soup tureen.

I no longer announce the start of soup season, as the kids run from the room, scooping up all the takeout menus they can find in the kitchen junk drawer. I will probably be opening up cans of watery chicken noodle for the rest of my life. I cannot be trusted. I don't know my habanera from a hole in the wall.

I have learned that the process of cooking can be more important than the result. The essence of family togetherness is sitting down at the table, sharing stories about our day. Would you like to come over and taste some of my flavorful microwave French Onion Soup? It's easy. You just take some onions . . . or are they shallots?

Fast French Onion Soup

Once you find a way to cut down on your onion tears, you'll have no problem mixing up a batch of your own onion soup. Would you invite me over?

2 tablespoons vegetable oil

2 medium onions, peeled and cut into ¼-inch slices (see Preparation Tip)

3 cans (14 ounces each) ready-to-serve beef broth

2 cups water

¼ teaspoon black pepper

⅓ cup dry red wine

¼ cup grated Parmesan cheese

1 In a medium skillet, heat the oil over medium-high heat. Sauté the onions for 10 to 15 minutes, until browned.

2 Place the onions in a large saucepan and combine with the beef broth, water, and pepper. Reduce the heat to low and simmer for about 20 minutes.

3 Mix in the wine and cheese and continue cooking over low heat until mixed through. Serve immediately or keep warm until ready to serve.

Preparation Tip: *There are many ideas for preventing tears when slicing onions—some are pretty wild! Here are a few of the more reasonable and effective ones:*

• *Peel onions under cold running water.*

• *Cut off the root end of the onion last.*

• *Whole onions shouldn't be stored in the refrigerator, but since a cold onion is less likely to make you cry than one at room temperature, put onions in the fridge to get cold before cutting.*

Serving Tip: *Serve topped with a few homemade croutons, or place in microwave-safe bowls, top with some shredded Gruyere cheese and heat in the microwave until the cheese melts. Your family won't be able to say anything but "Ooh-la-la!"*

Macaroni and Cheese Soup

This hearty dish was always a favorite of my kids, and it's sure to be a favorite of yours, too. I bet thoughts of this soup in their lunch thermoses will keep them attentive all through their morning classes!

SERVES
6 to 8

1 In a soup pot, bring the water to a boil over high heat. Stir in the peas and carrots and the macaroni, reserving the cheese packet. Cover and boil for 5 minutes; do not drain.

2 Add the remaining ingredients, including the reserved cheese packet. Reduce the heat to medium, cover, and simmer for 10 minutes, or until hot and creamy, stirring occasionally.

2½ cups water

1 package (10 ounces) frozen peas and carrots, thawed

1 package (7¼ ounces) macaroni and cheese mix

4 cups (1 quart) milk

1 cup (4 ounces) shredded sharp Cheddar cheese

1½ teaspoons salt

½ teaspoon black pepper

Serving Tip: *This makes a great lunch or light dinner with Deli Wraps or another favorite sandwich. Check out how great it looks on page 41.*

Throw-Together Chicken Vegetable Soup

SERVES 8 to 10

A big bowl of chicken soup is welcome any time. With this one, you can take some leftover veggies and chicken, toss 'em in a big pot, and in about 15 minutes you'll have a hearty, comforting soup that disappears even quicker than it goes together!

10 cups water

10 regular or low-sodium chicken bouillon cubes

3 cups shredded cooked chicken

1 package (16 ounces) frozen mixed vegetables, thawed

1/2 teaspoon black pepper

1. In a soup pot, add the water to the bouillon cubes and bring to a boil over medium-high heat. Boil until the bouillon cubes have dissolved, stirring occasionally.

2. Add the remaining ingredients and return to a boil. Reduce the heat to medium-low and simmer for 10 to 15 minutes, or until the vegetables are tender.

Timesaving Tip: *This sure is an excellent way to use up leftover chicken. And if you have leftover pasta or rice, add some to make this a heartier soup.*

Healthy Hint:

My grandchildren love taking soup in a thermos for school lunches, and I love that, especially with this one, they're getting loads of goodness in every serving. My oldest granddaughter even loves having soup for breakfast. I can't argue with her about that, since it's a healthy start to her day!

Chef's Salad Skewers

It's not easy to find a portable lunch, so I created this special one for when you and the kids are on the go.

SERVES 6

1. Place each slice of turkey on a flat surface then top each with one slice of ham, one slice of cheese, and one slice of roast beef.

2. Starting at the narrow end, roll up jelly-roll-style and slice each roll into three equal pieces. Alternately thread each skewer with two pieces each of the meat and cheese roll, the lettuce and tomato chunks.

3. Serve immediately, or cover and chill until ready to serve. Drizzle with your favorite salad dressing before serving.

Did You Know . . . *that there's a really easy way to keep salad chilled on your serving table? Fill a large bowl with a small amount of water and freeze. When ready to serve, place the salad in a smaller bowl and place that one in the large bowl. Ta da! Cool, crisp salad all throughout your party!*

4 slices (¼ pound) deli turkey

4 slices (¼ pound) deli ham

4 slices (2 ounces) Swiss *or* yellow Cheddar cheese

4 slices (¼ pound) deli roast beef

1 small head iceberg lettuce, cut into 12 chunks

1 large tomato, cut into 12 chunks

6 (10-inch) skewers

55

Pepper-Jack Quesadillas

MAKES 5 QUESADILLAS

If it's got cheese in it, you know the kids'll love it! And what could be easier than a quesadilla? Mmm!

2 ½ cups (10 ounces) shredded Monterey Jack-pepper cheese

10 (10-inch) flour tortillas

2 ½ teaspoons vegetable oil

1. Sprinkle ½ cup of the cheese over each of 5 tortillas and top with the remaining tortillas, making sandwiches.

2. In a large nonstick skillet, heat ½ teaspoon oil over medium heat. Place 1 "tortilla sandwich" in the skillet and cook for 3 to 4 minutes, or until the cheese is melted, turning halfway through the cooking.

3. Remove to a covered platter and continue with the remaining tortilla sandwiches until all are cooked. Cut each finished quesadilla into 4 wedges and serve.

Serving Tip: *These are great as is, but go ahead and offer toppings of sour cream, salsa, and sliced jalapeño peppers.*

·SNACKS·

Strawberry Cream Dip

For a quick and healthy snack, nothing fits the bill like fresh fruit. And when you cut it up and serve it with this dip, nobody can resist it.

MAKES
1½
CUPS

1 In a medium bowl, with an electric beater on medium speed, beat the cream cheese until creamy.

2 Add the yogurt and jam; continue beating until smooth. Cover and chill for at least one hour before serving.

1 package (8 ounces)
   cream cheese, softened
½ cup vanilla yogurt
½ cup strawberry jam

Option: *Substitute your favorite flavor jam or preserves for the strawberry jam.*

Healthy Hint:
Use reduced-fat cream cheese and low-fat yogurt, and serve with fresh-cut chunks of cantaloupe, honeydew, or pineapple, and apple slices and whole strawberries. It all works!

Roasted Red Pepper Hummus

MAKES 2½ CUPS

Hummus is a versatile spread that's available in the deli department of most supermarkets, but there's nothing like homemade. It's easy as 1–2–3, and beats those store-bought versions by a mile.

2 cans (15 ounces each) garbanzo beans (chickpeas), rinsed and drained, with ⅓ cup liquid reserved

1 jar (12 ounces) roasted red peppers, drained

3 garlic cloves

2 tablespoons fresh lemon juice

2 tablespoons olive oil

1 teaspoon ground cumin

1 teaspoon salt

1 In a food processor, combine all the ingredients, including the reserved garbanzo bean liquid. Process until the mixture is smooth and no lumps remain, scraping down the sides of the bowl as needed.

2 Serve immediately, or cover and chill until ready to use.

Option: It's easy to make this in a number of different flavors. If you'd prefer this plain, eliminate the roasted peppers. Of course, you could mix some chopped ripe olives, a bit of pesto sauce, or other favorite flavorings into the plain version. Any flavor that you enjoy will be a winner!

Healthy Hint:

Beans are high on the food pyramid as a "beaneficial" source of fiber, so this rich and creamy spread makes a great staple in almost any healthy meal plan.

Pepperoni Pizza Dip

SERVES
6 to 8

Ever heard the expression, "That was so good, I could have eaten the bowl?" Well, sometimes we can do just that. That's right, we can serve food in edible containers. The most popular one is a crunchy bread bowl to hold almost anything from thick and creamy soups to hearty dips like this one.

1 jar (28 ounces) spaghetti sauce

2 cups (8 ounces) shredded mozzarella cheese

1 package (3 1/2 ounces) sliced pepperoni, chopped

1/2 teaspoon garlic powder

1/2 teaspoon dried oregano

1 can (2 1/4 ounces) sliced black olives (optional)

1 (1-pound) round Italian bread, unsliced

1. In a medium saucepan, combine all the ingredients except the bread over low heat. Cook for 25 to 30 minutes, or until smooth and creamy, stirring occasionally.

2. Meanwhile, slice the top off the bread and hollow it out, reserving the insides and cutting it into chunks. Pour warm dip into the bread bowl and serve with bread chunks.

Preparation Tip: *It's a good idea to cut a second loaf of bread into chunks to make sure you have enough for dipping, and when you get to the bottom . . . go ahead and eat the "bowl"!*

Healthy Hint:

Make edible bowls out of red and yellow bell peppers for serving veggie dips, and red and green cabbage leaves for serving salads. The more different-colored foods we eat, the more vitamins we get!

Swiss-Onion Spread

This is definitely not your ordinary party or snack spread. It's sure to be a conversation starter at your next get-together!

MAKES
3
CUPS

1. Preheat the oven to 325°F. Coat a 9-inch pie plate with nonstick cooking spray.

2. In a large bowl, combine all the ingredients; mix well and spoon into the pie plate.

3. Bake for 25 to 30 minutes, or until golden and heated through.

1 package (10 ounces) frozen chopped onions, thawed and well drained

2½ cups (10 ounces) shredded Swiss cheese

1 cup mayonnaise

1 tablespoon Dijon mustard

⅛ teaspoon black pepper

Serving Tip: *This is terrific served with crackers, thick-sliced pumpernickel bread, or even celery sticks as a go-along with soup or salad.*

Full Circle

BY ELLEN JAVERNICK

I'm making pizzelles today. They're the perfectly round anise-flavored Italian cookies made by squeezing and cooking a sweet batter in something that looks a bit like a waffle iron. I learned to make pizzelles more than forty years ago . . . the first Christmas after I married into an Italian family. Grandma Castiliano led me through the process.

First, we melted the shortening. "In the old country," she explained, "we used lard from the pigs we butchered ourselves, and the anise seeds we added for the licorice flavoring grew on bushes on the hillsides beside our house."

The anise Grandma and I used came from the store, but the eggs didn't. She insisted that we needed to collect fresh ones from Aunt Josephine's henhouse across the way. The recipe called for twenty eggs. Grandma weighed the eggs in her hands and shook her head. "Too small." We needed three more to make the batter just the right consistency. I cracked the eggs while she mixed in the sugar. "Northern Italians," she bragged, "never use baking powder in their pizzelles. Good eggs are what make the cookies rise." We added the flour a little at a time until the dough was "not too thick, and not too thin."

While we stirred and stirred and stirred, the pizzelle iron was heating up. Grandma loved her new electric iron. When she'd first come to the United States, she'd had to cook the pizzelles over a wood-burning stove

64

with a hand iron. She'd kept it to show her daughter-in-laws. It looked like a pair of round, flat-faced scissors. It had been hard, she explained, to know just how much batter to add . . . too much and it squished out and dropped into the fire . . . too little and the cookies weren't round.

It wasn't even easy to use the electric iron. My first attempts ranged between burned and battery, but by the end of the morning most of my pizzelles at least looked presentable. Grandma said she was proud of me. I was proud of myself!

The following December, a box from Grandma and Grandpa arrived in the mail. The label said, "Open Before Christmas." I did and discovered my very own pizzelle iron. Every year since then, I've made pizzelles. I make them for friends and for the neighbors, for church bake sales and family weddings. The year our youngest son was due in December, I squeezed the iron together extra hard as I counted the minutes between contractions. When our oldest son was in kindergarten, he wanted to make "waffle cookies" for his teacher. We did, and for all the following Christmases our children gave them as gifts to their teachers. The year Grandpa died in November, I made some for his funeral dinner. When Grandma moved into the nursing home, I made them for her to give to her caregivers.

And as each of our children has married, I've mailed them, for their first Christmas, a pizzelle iron along with Grandma's recipe . . . and the admonition not to use baking powder. Pizzelle irons have changed. They've gotten fancier. They make several cookies at one time, and miracle of miracles, a light flashes on some of the newest ones to tell you when to open the iron to remove the cookies.

But in our family the tradition has not changed. Today I am making the pizzelles with my son because his wife is in the military in Afghanistan. Their baby is watching from the highchair beside us. She says "egg" each time we add one to the bowl. She wrinkles her nose in appreciation as the faint anise odor wafts from the edges of the iron. She claps when we open the iron and take out yet another perfect pizzelle.

Spinach Artichoke Dip

MAKES 3 CUPS This has become a classic party or anytime favorite that can be served with veggie sticks, your favorite crackers, or, my favorite, light, homemade pita crisps. Check 'em out on page 68.

1 package (10 ounces) frozen chopped spinach, thawed and squeezed dry

1 package (8 ounces) cream cheese, softened

3/4 cup grated Parmesan cheese

1/4 cup mayonnaise

1 teaspoon fresh lemon juice

1/4 teaspoon ground red pepper

1/4 teaspoon garlic powder

1 can (14 ounces) artichoke hearts, drained and chopped

1 Preheat the oven to 350°F. Coat a 1-quart casserole dish with nonstick cooking spray.

2 In a medium bowl, combine all the ingredients except the artichoke hearts; beat until well blended. Stir in the artichoke hearts then spoon into the casserole dish.

3 Bake for 30 to 35 minutes, or until heated through and the edges are golden. Serve immediately.

Preparation Tip: *For smaller gatherings, divide the uncooked mixture into smaller casserole dishes, wrap them well, and keep them on hand in the freezer. That way, you can always heat up a treat for last-minute guests.*

Itsy Bitsy Pizza Bagels

Your kids will be in their glory when you tell them they're going to make their own individual pizzas. Ask them which is more fun: making them or eating them!

MAKES
20
MINI PIZZAS

1 Preheat the oven to 350°F.

2 Split the bagels in half and spread 1 teaspoon sauce on each half. Sprinkle each half with 1 heaping teaspoon mozzarella cheese and 1 slice of pepperoni or mushroom and place on a foil-lined cookie sheet.

3 Bake for 10 to 12 minutes, or until the cheese is melted.

1 bag (9 ounces) frozen miniature bagels, thawed

$^1/_2$ cup pizza *or* spaghetti sauce

1 cup (4 ounces) shredded mozzarella cheese

20 slices pepperoni (1 ounce) *or* 1 jar (2$^1/_2$ ounces) mushroom stems and pieces, drained

Preparation Tip: *Keep the basic ingredients on hand for making this quick snack or lunch.*

Garlic Pita Crisps

SERVES 12 to 16

These crisps are the perfect partners for plain or Roasted Red Pepper Hummus (page 60). They make a crispy treat all by themselves, and also a light base for practically any of your favorite dips and spreads, so give 'em a try!

6 (6-inch) whole-wheat pita breads

Nonstick cooking spray

2 tablespoons garlic powder

1 Preheat the oven to 350°F.

2 Cut each pita into 8 equal wedges. Separate each wedge into 2 pieces.

3 Coat both sides of the pita wedges lightly with the cooking spray and place in a single layer on large rimmed baking sheets; sprinkle with garlic powder.

4 Bake for 15 minutes, or until golden and crisp.

5 Allow the crisps to cool; serve immediately, or store in an airtight container until ready to use.

Option: These tasty little crisps can easily be made in other flavors, so it's fun to make a selection that you can mix and match with your various party dips. Here's an example: Spread ¼ cup prepared pesto sauce then 2 tablespoons freshly grated Parmesan cheese evenly over the pita wedges and bake for 8 to 10 minutes, or until golden and crisp.

Pizza Chips

Keep a bag of these savory snacks in your desk drawer for taking the edge off until lunchtime or any other mealtime.

1 Preheat the oven to 375°F.

2 In a small bowl, combine the butter and spaghetti sauce mix; mix well.

3 Spread evenly over one side of the tortillas then sprinkle with the Parmesan cheese. Cut each tortilla into 8 wedges and place on baking sheets.

4 Bake for 8 to 10 minutes, or until the chips are golden and crispy.

½ cup (1 stick) butter, melted

1 package (1¼ ounces) dry spaghetti sauce mix

10 (8-inch) flour tortillas

¼ cup grated Parmesan cheese

Serving Tip: *These are terrific as is or served with warm marinara sauce for dunking.*

Fruit Roll Sushi

MAKES about 30 PIECES

When you tell the kids you're serving sushi as an after-school snack, there are sure to be cries of, "Ooh, I'm not eating that!" But once they hear it's fruit roll sushi, made with all the things they love, the cries will change to, "Yummy!" and "More, please!"

1 tablespoon butter

12 marshmallows

2 cups crispy toasted rice cereal

4 (4½-inch) square fruit roll-ups (½ ounce each)

6 assorted licorice *or* fruit twist sticks, cut in half crosswise

1. In a medium saucepan, melt the butter over low heat. Add the marshmallows and stir until completely melted. Remove from the heat and stir in the cereal until completely coated.

2. On a flat surface, unroll the fruit roll-ups. Spread equal amounts of the cereal mixture over each roll-up, covering the entire surface and packing the mixture flat.

3. Place 3 different-colored licorice or fruit twists in the center of each and roll tightly into a log, sealing where the edges meet. Squeeze the rolls gently to secure. Trim the ends and slice with a serrated knife into ½-inch pieces. Serve, or store in an airtight container until ready to serve.

Preparation Tip: *To give your snacks the most variety and color, use different-colored and -flavored fruit roll-ups and licorice or fruit twist sticks. And if you can't find different-colored licorice, you can even use gummy worms.*

70

Rainy Day Rescue

BY JUNE WILLIAMS

Rain had been falling relentlessly for days. The kids were bored, I was frustrated, and fights were inevitable. What could I do to break the monotony?

While searching my childhood memories, I came up with a fun activity I'd always loved. We'd have an old-fashioned taffy pull. I leafed through my tattered cookbook and found an easy recipe. What luck! I had everything I needed on hand.

Soon the biggest kettle in the kitchen was bubbling and a sweet smell filled the air. The kids, who were at war just a moment before, stood beside the stove awaiting my instructions.

"This is the hard part," I told them. "We have to wait for the candy to cook and cool before we can start pulling taffy."

Once the boiling mixture reached the right temperature, I poured it into shallow pans to cool. Mitch and Alison stood over the steaming pans, sniffing huge, mint-scented breaths. The cooling process takes time—about fifty repetitions of "Is it ready yet?"

I kept poking the thickening candy with my finger until I judged it cool enough for pulling. "Butter your hands," I called. "It's time to pull!"

I wadded the first ball. It was a little too hot, but we had to hurry. Cooling means hardening, and we wanted our taffy soft and chewy. I stretched out the squishy ball of taffy and handed one end to my eight-year-old son. We pulled and twisted, folded and pulled again. Once he had the hang of it, I handed my end to his four-year-old sister. While they worked their half of the batch, I started kneading, stretching and folding the remainder.

Handling warm, sticky stuff is just plain fun, and we were all laughing as we worked the candy. A couple of times the kids stretched too far. The string of candy broke, and bits of goo dripped to the floor. Hands had to be re-buttered often, as sticky won out over greasy time and again. The mess only contributed to the fun. Nobody was bored or angry now. We were candy-makers together.

Before long, all the taffy was pulled to a soft, green color. We stretched out two long strands on buttered waxed paper. I cut the candy into bite-sized pieces, and the kids wrapped each piece in waxed paper and tossed it into my biggest mixing bowl. Of course, a few warm pieces slipped into eager mouths, but the bowl was overflowing when all the taffy was wrapped.

Mitch and Alison rushed into the bathroom to wash their hands all the way to their shoulders, while I started soaking sugary pots and pans and scrubbing the very sticky kitchen floor.

When Mac opened the back door that evening, he was greeted with cries of, "Dad! Dad! We made our own taffy!" Despite the mess I'd had to clean up, I smiled. Messy teamwork beat neat and tidy fighting any day.

While taffy pulls never became a frequent activity in our house, they sure came in handy on desperate, rainy days.

Cinnamon-Sugar Pretzels

MAKES
12
PRETZELS

Why settle for plain old pretzels when it's this easy to enjoy fresh piping-hot ones coated with cinnamon and sugar? Yup, they're a sweet "twist" on an old favorite.

1 package (11 ounces) refrigerated soft bread stick dough

¼ cup sugar

¼ teaspoon ground cinnamon

2 tablespoons butter, melted

1 Preheat the oven to 375°F. Coat a baking sheet with nonstick cooking spray.

2 Unroll the bread sticks and separate into 12 strips. Twist each strip into a pretzel shape and place on the baking sheet.

3 In a small bowl, combine the sugar and cinnamon. Brush the pretzels with the melted butter then sprinkle with the sugar-cinnamon mixture.

4 Bake for 13 to 15 minutes, or until golden. Serve immediately.

Option: *No, these don't only have to be sweet. You can top 'em with kosher salt for a traditional pretzel, or with a mix of garlic powder and herbs in olive oil.*

Granola Break-Up

Looking for an inexpensive gift you can make yourself? Here's the answer! With just 3 ingredients and very little time, you can make this perfect snack that also works great as an ice cream or yogurt topper.

MAKES
8
CUPS

1 Preheat the oven to 300°F. Coat a large rimmed baking sheet with nonstick cooking spray.

2 In a large bowl, combine all the ingredients; mix well. Spread the mixture evenly over the baking sheet and bake for 35 to 40 minutes, or until golden. Allow to cool for 5 minutes then invert onto a clean work surface. Allow to cool completely then break into bite-sized pieces. Serve, or store in an airtight container.

1 box (16 ounces) granola with almonds and raisins

1½ cups lightly salted peanuts

1 can (14 ounces) sweetened condensed milk

Option: *Go ahead and use your favorite granola—with or without raisins and nuts—or add additional raisins and/or nuts of your choice.*

Nutty Caramel Corn

MAKES 13 CUPS

The average American consumes between 50 and 60 quarts of popcorn a year. And I'd say it's a good bet that consumption of popcorn will go up in your household after they get a taste of this one!

1 cup packed light brown sugar

½ cup (1 stick) butter

¼ cup honey

1 teaspoon vanilla extract

12 cups popped plain popcorn

1 can (12 ounces) unsalted mixed nuts

1 Preheat the oven to 250°F.

2 In a small saucepan, bring the brown sugar, butter, and honey to a boil over medium-high heat and cook for 5 minutes, stirring frequently.

3 Remove from the heat and add the vanilla; mix well.

4 In a large bowl, combine the popcorn and nuts. Pour the brown sugar mixture over the popcorn and nuts and stir until thoroughly coated. Spoon onto 2 ungreased large rimmed baking sheets and bake for 1 hour, stirring every 15 minutes.

5 Let cool completely, until crisp. Serve, or store in an airtight container until ready to serve.

Healthy Hint:

Finally, a snack that tastes great and is good for us! Popcorn is a whole-grain food that's low in calories (when made without hydrogenated oils and butter topping) and is a good source of fiber. The National Cancer Institute, the American Dental Association and the American Dietetic Association suggest popcorn as a sensible, versatile snack that fits into almost every meal plan.

Did You Know . . . *that plain, unbuttered popcorn makes great packing material for shipping cookies? Of course, this popcorn is something you'll want to wrap and send as a gift all by itself!*

Steak Pizzaiola

If you want to make a really good impression, it's no hassle to serve up this simple yet classic Italian recipe.

SERVES
2 to 4

1. Season the steaks on both sides with the onion powder, garlic powder, salt, and black pepper.

2. In a large skillet, heat the oil over medium-high heat. Brown the steaks for 2 minutes per side.

3. Reduce the heat to medium, and add the onion, bell pepper, and diced tomatoes to the skillet; cover and cook for 5 minutes.

4. Uncover the skillet and cook for 7 to 10 more minutes, or to desired doneness, turning the steaks halfway through cooking.

Serving Tip: *For great steak sandwiches, thinly slice these steaks and serve on sandwich rolls topped with the vegetables and sauce.*

2 boneless beef strip steaks (8 to 10 ounces each), 1 inch thick

1/4 teaspoon onion powder

1/4 teaspoon garlic powder

1/4 teaspoon salt

1/4 teaspoon black pepper

2 tablespoons olive oil

1 medium-sized onion, thinly sliced

1 medium-sized green bell pepper, cut into thin strips

1 can (14 1/2 ounces) Italian-style diced tomatoes, undrained

Marinated Steak Nachos

When you're in the mood for steak but don't want a heavy main course, try these steak nachos. They're satisfying and quick enough for a hearty lunch or dinner!

½ cup lemon juice

2 tablespoons minced garlic

1 tablespoon dried oregano

1 tablespoon ground cumin

1 teaspoon salt

1 tablespoon black pepper

1 (1½-pound) beef flank steak

1 package (14 ounces) tortilla chips

2 cups (8 ounces) shredded Colby Jack cheese blend

2 large tomatoes, seeded and chopped

3 scallions, thinly sliced

1. In a 9" x 13" baking dish, combine the lemon juice, garlic, oregano, cumin, salt, and pepper. Add the flank steak, turning to coat completely. Cover and marinate in the refrigerator for 30 minutes.

2. Preheat the broiler. Place steak on a rimmed baking sheet; discard marinade. Broil for 8 to 9 minutes per side for medium, or until desired doneness beyond that.

3. Allow to cool for 10 minutes. Place on a cutting board and cut across the grain into thin slices then cut into 1-inch pieces. Spread the tortilla chips over two large rimmed baking sheets then top evenly with the sliced steak and sprinkle with the cheese. Reduce the oven temperature to 350°F. and bake for 5 to 6 minutes, or until the cheese has melted.

4. Remove the nachos from the oven and slide onto a large platter, if desired; sprinkle with the tomatoes and scallions. Serve immediately.

Option: *Use more or less cheese, or even a different kind, and sprinkle finished nachos with chopped green chilies, jalapeño peppers, olives, salsa, sour cream, or other toppings.*

BY MARIAN GORMLEY

As with most families, dinnertime at our house has always been a time to reconnect with each other, a time to talk about the day's events or schedules. Not long ago, however, I found myself longing for deeper, fuller communication with my family. I wanted us to share our feelings about the events of the day rather than just relating what happened. I wanted to hear the ups and downs, the joys, the challenges and accomplishments each of us experienced throughout our days. After much contemplation, I began a new ritual.

During dinner, my husband, Pat, and I, along with our ten-year-old twins Tara and Jake, share a few feelings we experienced during the day. At first, I encountered some understandable resistance from my husband after an exhausting day at the office. I think it initially seemed like more work to him. He'd give me a "not-this-again-I've-had-a-long-day" look. On those days, the children would go first, and then they'd exclaim, "Daddy, Daddy! It's your turn now! Tell us some feelings about your day!" These days, Pat actually enjoys this way to connect with us, and he sees it as an opportunity to teach our children lessons about everyday life.

Since I considered our children to be generally in tune with their feelings, I was surprised when we first began this ritual. Tara or Jake would often say, "Ummm . . . I can't really think of any feelings I had today." I'd ask, "How did you feel when you saw your friend so-and-so today?" or "How did you feel when you took that test you studied for last night?"

After we all became more comfortable talking about our feelings, I noticed that more often than not they began with "I was happy when . . ." or "I was sad when . . ." Realizing that there are so many more words to express feelings, I found a poster for the kitchen that had faces and expressions with various feelings noted underneath. This helped the children to expand their "feelings vocabulary," e.g., anxious, proud, discouraged, excited, frustrated, surprised. We discussed what these words meant and slowly began incorporating them into our discussions.

There are occasions now when dinner is over before we realize that one of us hasn't yet had an opportunity to share a feeling. I'll simply say, "Hey, we didn't hear from Tara yet" or "What about me? Does anyone want to hear one of my feelings today?" and then we all sit together a few more minutes.

We've been sharing feelings at dinner for over a year now. By sharing more intimate details of our days, we are reaping noticeable rewards. Having each of us take a few moments to explore how we felt at some point during the day often uncovers a lot more than any of us realized. These discussions at dinner provide opportunities for sharing accomplishments, offering congratulations, recognizing and easing anxieties, and asking for and offering support. Also, the rest of the evening seems to go more smoothly when we know the type of day each person has had.

We are getting to know one another on a deeper level, and we've come to explore and respect our own and each other's feelings more. This has helped Pat and me not only to become better parents, but also better marriage partners to each other. Sharing these dinnertime feelings and listening to their parents' feelings on a regular basis has also made Jake and Tara more empathetic and thoughtful.

Not long ago I had lunch plans with a close family friend whose husband had recently passed away. On the morning of the lunch, I told the kids that I would be at my office in the morning and then would be meeting Wendy for lunch. Jake had complained of a brief stomachache before school, but felt fine after breakfast. During lunch, I received a phone call from Jake. "Mom, are you at your meeting or your special lunch with Wendy?" When I told him I was with Wendy, he responded, "Mom, you go ahead and finish your lunch. I'll lie down in the clinic until you get here. Don't hurry because I know Wendy needs you a lot more than I do right now."

My heart went out to him. I wanted to hug him, not only because he wasn't feeling well, but because of his thoughtful consideration of my need to spend time with our dear friend.

Big Burger

SERVES 6

You won't hear "Hamburgers again?!" from your family when you serve up this big burger that everybody can share. Instead, you'll hear, "Can you make that fun burger again, Mom?!"

1 1/2 pounds lean ground beef

1 small onion, finely chopped

1 teaspoon salt

1 teaspoon black pepper

1/4 pound Cheddar cheese, sliced

4 iceberg or romaine lettuce leaves

1 (8-inch) round loaf Italian or white bread, cut horizontally in half

1 Preheat the oven to 375°F. Coat a 9-inch pie plate with nonstick cooking spray.

2 In a large bowl, combine the ground beef, onion, salt, and pepper; mix well and form into a large hamburger patty. Place in the pie plate and bake for 30 minutes.

3 Remove from the oven and top with the cheese slices. Return to the oven and bake for 5 to 8 minutes, or until no pink remains in the ground beef and the cheese is melted.

4 Place the lettuce leaves over the bottom half of the bread then top with the burger. Replace the top of the bread, cut into wedges, and serve.

Healthy Hint:

We can pack more vitamins and nutrients into our diets by using darker-colored lettuces. Instead of making sandwiches and salads with iceberg, try romaine or other leafy green varieties.

Serving Tip: *Before cutting this into wedges, you can top it with your favorite condiments like ketchup, mustard, mayonnaise, or pickles—or, if everybody likes something different, serve the toppers on the side.*

84

Fast Taco Pie

What a neat idea this is! We make and serve it right from the same skillet. The family will love how tasty it is, and you'll love how easy it is to make and clean up!

SERVES
4 to 6

1. In a large nonstick skillet, cook the beef over medium-high heat for 6 to 7 minutes, or until browned, stirring frequently; drain off excess liquid.

2. Stir in the refried beans and salsa, breaking up the mixture with the back of a spoon. Bring to a boil, reduce the heat to low, and simmer for 5 minutes, or until well combined and heated through, stirring frequently. Remove the skillet from the heat, scrape down the sides with a spatula, and smooth the mixture evenly in the skillet.

3. Arrange the lettuce, tomatoes, cheese, and sour cream in concentric circles (one inside the next) on top of the beef mixture and serve immediately.

1 pound lean ground beef

1 can (16 ounces) refried beans

1 cup salsa

2 cups shredded iceberg *or* chopped romaine lettuce

2 large tomatoes, chopped

1 cup (4 ounces) shredded Cheddar cheese

$\frac{1}{2}$ cup sour cream

Serving Tip: *If you prefer, remove the beef mixture to a platter then layer with the lettuce, tomatoes, cheese, and sour cream.*

Muffin Tin Meat Loaves

MAKES 12 MUFFINS By making meat loaf in muffin tins, you reduce the cooking time . . . which means that dinner can be on the table quicker. Now, isn't that great news?!

1½ pounds lean ground beef

1 egg, slightly beaten

1½ cups shredded zucchini (about 1 medium zucchini)

1 teaspoon dried Italian seasoning

½ teaspoon salt

1 cup bread crumbs

¼ cup ketchup

1 Preheat the oven to 400°F.

2 In a large bowl, combine all the ingredients except the ketchup, mixing lightly but thoroughly. Place about ⅓ cup of the beef mixture into each of 12 medium muffin cups, pressing lightly; spread ketchup over the tops.

3 Bake for 20 minutes, or until no pink remains and the juices run clear.

Option: *If you want, you can use yellow squash in place of the zucchini . . . or some of both!*

Healthy Hint:

Not only is this a quick dinner, but it's a great way for kids of all ages to get everything they need in an all-in-one muffin!

BAD (POT) LUCK

BY ROBIN EHRLICHMAN WOODS

Although our family had branches in France, Germany, England and Ireland, I never claimed any ethnic recipe as my own. Two fussy eaters limited my repertoire to pasta or boxed macaroni and cheese, with never-ending requests for junk food. I strived to recreate the special dishes made with such love and expertise by my Nana, and searched everywhere to find a recipe that could match her tsimmes. I knew that it was a complicated, costly dish to prepare, but I wanted to impress our friends at the annual International Potluck Dinner and Raffle.

The preparation of tsimmes is in and of itself a very big deal. After finding a recipe in a holiday cookbook, I went shopping for the ingredients: beef brisket, carrots, apricots, prunes, white and sweet potatoes. I also needed to purchase a large disposable aluminum pan to cook and serve it in. I followed the recipe exactly, since I was not secure enough to improvise with any of the directions or ingredients. Boy, was this a pain to prepare! Cut up the beef, put it in braising liquid in a Dutch oven on the stove. Slice the carrots and apricots. Dice the sweet potatoes and prunes, and then assemble the spices and garnishes for the dish.

Once the beef brisket was cooked to supposed perfection (if that were possible), I added the remaining ingredients to the pan. It did smell good, and the colors of the beef, carrots, apricots and sweet potatoes were eye-catching. At last, the timer's bell rang. With great anticipation, I opened the oven door for a quick peek. I stirred the ingredients around one last time and turned off the heat. Armed with two potholder gloves, I reached in to lift out the steaming, redolent tsimmes. As soon as I lifted the pan away from the oven rack, it tilted crazily, depositing the ingredients into the space between the oven and the door. I couldn't stop it from happening—it was like lava erupting from a volcano. I stood there, tears in my eyes, and watched my dinner contribution slowly trickle down from the oven door to the floor.

What had I done wrong? When I purchased the large, disposable aluminum pan, I noticed that it had "Support Bottom" printed inside. I remember giggling about this—about supporting our own bottoms while cooking—then, it dawned on me. "Support Bottom" meant that the pan would collapse if it were lifted by the sides only. I had tried to put one of my hands at the bottom of the pan, but it was so large, I couldn't manage it.

After drying my eyes, I began the task of trying to rescue my tsimmes. I was faced with a moral dilemma. There was a small amount of the beef left in the pan, but most of the dish was on the oven door and kitchen floor. Should I scoop up the good stuff from the oven door and place it back in the pan? After all, it hadn't hit the floor, and I had cleaned the oven the night before, always a bad idea. Clean ovens attract disasters. It was too late to start the dish once again. I could have paid a caterer to do it for just a few more dollars.

I couldn't show up empty-handed, but perhaps I could rescue the remaining beef and scant apricots, carrots, prunes and sweet potatoes sticking to the bottom of the pan. What would I call it? Surprise stew? I made a frantic call to a friend who would be attending the dinner with her children. After I told her the story of all my hard work and what had happened, she said, "That's why no one in their right mind makes it anymore."

I wondered if I would be struck by lightning if I just scooped up whatever was salvageable and arranged it nicely on a serving platter. My friend assured me that no one would be the wiser, so I rescued more than half of the tsimmes, garnished it and placed it in a platter to carry to school. I used my son as a taste-tester, and he said that the dish was "interesting," leading me to believe that it was either fabulous or so weird that the other parents would be intrigued by it. I almost caved in and ordered three pizzas to go, but I had my Supermom image to protect.

I didn't tell a soul what had happened during the preparation of this dish. Much to my surprise, I received rave reviews and kudos for my hard work. Nana would be pleased. Every morsel of it was eaten, and when three or four people mentioned they would love more, well . . . I did just happen to have 4 to 6 servings on my previously spotless kitchen floor . . .

89

Slow Cooker Sweet-and-Sour Meatballs

SERVES 12 to 15

We usually think of these as a treat that we can only enjoy at holiday parties. Why wait? Your family will love 'em for dinner tonight!

1 jar (9 to 10 ounces) sweet-and-sour sauce

¼ cup packed light brown sugar

3 tablespoons soy sauce

½ teaspoon garlic powder

½ teaspoon black pepper

2½ pounds frozen meatballs

2 bell peppers (1 red and 1 green), chopped

1 can (20 ounces) pineapple chunks, drained

1 Place all ingredients in a 4-quart or larger slow cooker; stir gently then cover with the lid. Cook on low setting for 7 to 8 hours, or on high setting for 4 to 5 hours, until done.

2 Carefully remove the lid to allow steam to escape; serve.

Option: *Have a bit more time? Make your own meatballs instead of using frozen.*

Creamy Basil Pork Chops

They'll go "hog wild" over the creamy herb sauce that makes every mouthful of these juicy chops pure heaven.

SERVES 6

1 In a large skillet, heat 2 tablespoons olive oil over medium-high heat. Add the garlic and sauté for 1 to 2 minutes. Reduce the heat to medium, add the pork chops, and cook for 6 to 7 minutes per side, until brown on both sides.

2 Meanwhile, in a small bowl, combine the remaining 1 tablespoon olive oil, the basil, salt, and pepper. Add to the skillet 3 to 4 minutes before the chops are done, spreading the mixture around the skillet and turning the chops to coat with the basil mixture. When the chops are cooked through, remove to a serving plate and cover to keep warm.

3 Whisk the cream into the pan drippings for 2 to 3 minutes over medium heat, until the sauce thickens slightly. Pour the sauce over the cooked chops and serve immediately.

3 tablespoons olive oil, divided

4 garlic cloves, minced

6 (½-inch-thick) pork loin chops (2 pounds total), well trimmed

2 tablespoons chopped fresh basil (see Tip)

¼ teaspoon salt

¼ teaspoon black pepper

⅓ cup heavy cream *or* half-and-half

Timesaving Tip: *An easy way to chop fresh basil is really not to chop it at all, but to roll it up and snip it into thin strips with kitchen shears.*

91

Peachy Pork

SERVES 6

What an elegant dish this is! It's perfect for when you're having company, or when you want to treat your family like company!

1 cup peach preserves

¼ cup white vinegar

2 tablespoons Dijon mustard

2 tablespoons vegetable oil

2 pork tenderloins (about 2 pounds total)

¼ teaspoon salt

¼ teaspoon pepper

2 cups fresh peach slices *or* frozen peach slices, thawed

1 In a small bowl, stir together the preserves, vinegar, and mustard; set aside.

2 In a large skillet, heat the oil over medium-high heat. Season the tenderloins with salt and pepper, and add to the skillet. Cook for 4 to 5 minutes, turning to brown on all sides.

3 Reduce the heat to medium-low and add the reserved preserves mixture. Cover and simmer for 18 to 20 minutes, until no pink remains in the center of the pork, or to desired doneness.

4 Add the peaches to the skillet, and cook just until heated through. Slice and serve the tenderloins topped with peach sauce.

Healthy Hint:

Pork tenderloin is one of the leanest cuts available at the supermarket meat department. If trimmed, a single portion has only 1 gram of saturated fat. That's why it's such a healthy choice!

Serving Tip: *Serve warm slices of tenderloin topped with peach sauce over mixed salad greens and garnish with fresh raspberries for the exciting and novel contrast of hot and cold, savory and sweet.*

Peach Preserves

Oven-"Fried" Drumsticks

Crank up the heat, cook up a batch of this crunchy chicken and pair it with coleslaw for an indoor midwinter picnic the family will enjoy. No ants invited!

SERVES
4

1 Preheat the oven to 375°F. Coat a rimmed baking sheet with nonstick cooking spray.

2 Place the flour in a shallow dish. In a second shallow dish, beat the egg with the milk. In a third shallow dish, mix the crushed cereal with the seasonings.

3 Dip the chicken in the flour then into the egg mixture, followed by the cereal mixture, coating evenly with each. Arrange the chicken on the baking sheet and coat with nonstick cooking spray.

4 Bake for 25 minutes then turn the chicken and bake for 25 more minutes, or until the chicken is golden on the outside and no pink remains on the inside.

Nonstick cooking spray
¼ cup all-purpose flour
1 egg
¼ cup low-fat (1%) milk
1 cup coarsely crushed oven-toasted corn cereal
½ teaspoon dried oregano
½ teaspoon garlic powder
½ teaspoon onion powder
½ teaspoon paprika
½ teaspoon dried basil
½ teaspoon salt
¼ teaspoon black pepper
8 chicken drumsticks, skin removed

Healthy Hint:

With this one, we get the same great taste of the beloved American dish, but it's better for us, since it's made in the oven instead of a grease-filled fryer.

93

Ketchup WITH Kids

BY CRISTY TRANDAHL

"Kids, the dishwasher's broken again. Can you help me with the dishes just this once?" My six children groan in surround sound. A dozen eyes scan the dinner table: Sloppy ketchup-smeared plates, greasy, limp, leftover French fries, and pooled Italian dressing pollute its surface like an oil spill from an ocean liner. What a mess.

A year ago, our automatic dishwasher blew a circuit panel. "Struck by lightning," concluded the repairman, pulling his head from the heart of the machine. "Not worth repairing." Just my luck. Until we were able to purchase a new one, the kids and I would have to do dishes the old-fashioned way. Each of our four oldest children was assigned a day of the week. On Sundays I could be heard grumbling from mounds of dirty dishes, "If Sunday is the Lord's Day, shouldn't he do dishes today?"

Dishes duty in our busy home is no easy task. There are breakfast and dinner dishes for eight and lunch dishes for seven. After a few months of hand-washing dishes, my twelve-year-old complained, "I'm growing webbed hands from doing so many dishes! I'm becoming amphibious!"

The children had their individual ways of dealing with the demands of dishes day. One would stay ahead of the game, doing four or five "mini-loads" throughout the day. Others would procrastinate, only to spend a full two hours at bedtime shoveling through drifts of dishes. One child would beg breakfast cereal for every meal: "It's nutritious, economical and a cinch to clean up, Mom!" This was the same child who requested that we use paper products for eternity. But after unpleasant experiences with collapsed paper plates, snapped plastic silverware and leaky plastic cups, I put a nix on the disposable dinnerware.

Most of the time, I have to admit, cleanup was drudgery. But every once in a while, while wading through waves of grimy pots and pans, domestic transcendence occurred. Sometimes, the kids and I reviewed multiplication facts or conjugated verbs, (I do dishes, she does dishes, and they have done dishes.) Other times we'd discuss soccer or basketball games. ("Coach didn't start me in the last game. I was disappointed.")

After a few weeks, I noticed that my children were more willing to share their feelings with me while we scrubbed dishes together. Maybe it was the mind-numbing repetition, or the warm, soothing dishwater, or the side-by-side camaraderie. Whatever it was, I began to look forward to helping my children with their supper dishes. In those months of hand-washing dishes, I learned a lot about my kids.

"I want to be an audiologist when I grow up so I can help kids who can't hear well," my eight-year-old shared. She has hearing loss.

"Mom, today in history I read something about African-Americans not being able to go to the same schools as other kids. Did that really happen?" asked my ten-year-old.

"Mom, why did our dog have to die? Doesn't God care about my prayers?" inquired my six-year-old.

"Mom, some girls in middle school are dating already," informed my twelve-year-old.

"Look, Mom! I can snap my toes!" giggled my four-year-old.

Standing in front of the kitchen sink, I had time to notice that my first daughter was maturing into a young woman. She was, in fact, as tall as me. My second daughter has her dad's perfect nose and my cowlick. I discovered my third and fourth children could sing beautifully, and my fifth child has fingers like a pianist. Why had I not noticed that before? And my sixth, a toddler, displayed his vocabulary: "poon," "fowk," "nife" and "cup." Dishes gave me time to marvel at the beauty of my children.

Last month, my husband installed a brand-new dishwasher. It has a whisper quiet motor, an exceptionally high-energy efficiency rating and a stainless steel interior. There's a "time saver" feature and a "quick dry" cycle. The labor of meal cleanup is done in a snap now, and I'm grateful for the help. But the dishwasher's not as much fun to talk with as my children.

So, every once in a while, after a particularly sloppy supper like California burgers, French fries dripping with ketchup, Italian greens with dressing and strawberry sorbet, I'll fill the kitchen sink with warm, sudsy water, drag out the dish towels and tell a little white lie: "Kids, the dishwasher's broken again. Can you help me with dishes just this once?"

It's my time to catch up with the kids.

Asian Chicken Salad

SERVES 6 to 8

When most of us think about cabbage and salad, we think of coleslaw. Well, how 'bout making that team into something special that makes for a really fast meal?

2 tablespoons sesame oil

1/2 cup sesame seeds

4 garlic cloves, minced

2 pounds boneless, skinless chicken breasts, cut into 1/2-inch chunks

3/4 cup vegetable oil

1/2 cup sugar

1/4 cup soy sauce

1/4 cup white vinegar

1 head Napa (Chinese) cabbage, cut into bite-sized pieces

1/4 pound snow peas, trimmed

1. In a large skillet, heat the sesame oil over medium heat; sauté the sesame seeds and garlic for 2 to 3 minutes, or until the sesame seeds are golden.

2. Add the chicken, vegetable oil, sugar, soy sauce, and vinegar to the skillet, and cook for 4 to 5 minutes, or until no pink remains in the chicken.

3. Meanwhile, place the cabbage and snow peas in a large bowl or on a serving platter. Top with the cooked chicken mixture and toss until well coated. Serve immediately.

Healthy Hint:

To give this even more color, flavor, and nutrition, add a can of drained mandarin oranges to the salad.

Spicy Chicken 'n' Bean Skillet

Why make the kids eat take-out when you can prepare an ethnic treat they'll love this quickly at home?! (It's a lot healthier too!)

SERVES 3 to 4

1. Coat a large skillet with nonstick cooking spray; heat over medium heat. Add the chicken, onion, and garlic, and sauté for 5 to 6 minutes, stirring until the chicken is browned on all sides.

2. Stir in the beans, tomato, salsa, salt, and pepper. Cook for 1 to 2 minutes, or until heated through and no pink remains in the chicken.

3. Spoon over warm rice, if desired, and serve topped with a dollop of sour cream.

Garnishing Tip: *Make this more authentic by garnishing it with additional chopped onions and salsa, or shredded Cheddar cheese and cilantro.*

½ pound boneless, skinless chicken thighs, cut into ¾-inch chunks

1 small onion, chopped

1 teaspoon minced garlic

1 can (15 ounces) black or kidney beans, rinsed and drained

1 medium tomato, chopped

½ cup salsa

¼ teaspoon salt

¼ teaspoon black pepper

3 cups cooked rice (optional)

½ cup sour cream

Healthy Hint:

High in protein and fiber, and with significant anti-oxidant potential, black beans are a terrific addition to your family's menus. They'll love how great they taste in here too!

Chicken & Biscuits

Think comfort food has to take a long time to prepare and cook? Uh uh! It takes no time when you know what convenience items to keep on hand. And, speaking of time, wait 'til you see them come running for this one!

2 cups diced cooked chicken

1 package (16 ounces) frozen mixed vegetables

2 jars (12 ounces each) chicken gravy

1 large package (16.3 ounces) refrigerated buttermilk biscuits (8 biscuits)

1 Preheat the oven to 350°F. Coat a 9" x 13" baking dish with nonstick cooking spray.

2 In a large bowl, combine the chicken, vegetables, and gravy; mix well then spoon into the baking dish. Top with the biscuits.

3 Bake for 15 to 20 minutes, or until hot and bubbly, and the biscuits are golden.

Timesaving Tip: We're lucky that we have options for buying already-cooked chicken for recipes like these. Use either a package of diced cooked chicken, or dice it yourself using a store-bought rotisserie chicken. Nobody has to know that we didn't slave in the kitchen for hours!

98

Sweet-and-Sour Chicken

SERVES 6 to 8

This traditional Chinese dish includes loads of fresh veggies—and even a fruit—in a sauce the kids will love, so rack up those daily servings!

2 tablespoons vegetable oil

2 ½ pounds boneless, skinless chicken breasts, cut into thin strips

1 can (20 ounces) pineapple chunks in syrup, drained and liquid reserved

1 can (8 ounces) sliced water chestnuts, drained

1 cup fresh broccoli florets

1 medium-sized red bell pepper, cut into ¾-inch chunks

2 tablespoons soy sauce

1 tablespoon white vinegar

1 tablespoon ketchup

2 tablespoons cornstarch

2 tablespoons sugar

1 cup fresh snow peas, trimmed

1 Heat the oil in a large skillet or wok over high heat. Add the chicken and stir-fry for 4 to 5 minutes, or until no pink remains.

2 Add the pineapple chunks, water chestnuts, broccoli, and bell pepper. Stir-fry for 3 to 4 minutes, or until the vegetables are crisp-tender.

3 In a small bowl, combine the reserved pineapple juice, the soy sauce, vinegar, ketchup, cornstarch, and sugar; mix well. Stir into the skillet and cook for 3 minutes.

4 Add the snow peas and cook for 1 minute, or until the sauce has thickened. Serve immediately.

Garnishing Tip: *This looks even more colorful garnished with maraschino cherries.*

Timesaving Tip: *Pick up a package of fresh broccoli florets from your supermarket's produce department. That saves on the cutting and trimming.*

Skillet Chicken and Potatoes

When you make this easy skillet chicken dish and top it with mashed potatoes, it'll bring back memories of yesteryear. Aah, what comfort.

SERVES 4 to 6

1 In a large skillet, combine all the ingredients except the potatoes over high heat; mix well. Cook for 5 minutes, or until heated through, stirring frequently.

2 Remove from the heat and top with the hot mashed potatoes. Serve immediately.

Timesaving Tip: *You can use leftover potatoes, instant mashed potatoes, or even the refrigerated or frozen packaged ones that are oh-so-tasty and convenient . . . especially for dishes like this one!*

2 cups cubed cooked chicken

1 package (16 ounces) frozen mixed vegetables, thawed and drained

1 can (10¾ ounces) condensed cream of chicken soup

½ cup milk

¼ teaspoon onion powder

¼ teaspoon black pepper

4 cups hot mashed potatoes (see Tip)

101

My Sous-Chef

BY MARIAN GORMLEY

Before I had children, I thought families sat down at the dinner table and enjoyed peaceful, nutritious meals. Surely the efforts of the cook were always appreciated, and sometimes even applauded. To the contrary, I have since learned that children believe it a part of their job description to make mealtimes challenging.

Recently I realized that I had grown tired of answering the "What's for dinner?" question, especially with responses such as "I don't want that," "You know I don't like that," or "What else can I have instead?"

What was I doing wrong? I planned. I shopped. I cooked. I served new recipes, as well as old favorites. But the mealtime whining still occurred more often than I liked. What to do?

My seven-year-old daughter, Tara, asked, "Mom, why can't I ever pick what we are going to have for dinner?" I carefully considered her question and we all agreed on a new approach. One day a week, my children would alternate taking a turn not only planning the menu, but also assisting in meal preparation.

After discussing why balanced meals are important, Tara and I outlined a shopping list for her first special meal. At the market, Tara, brimming with enthusiasm, pushed the cart.

First, she carefully chose a pint of juicy, red strawberries "for a side dish." Then, she favored the shucked ears of corn on the cob neatly wrapped in plastic at double the cost. We discussed how unshucked corn was more economical and fun to prepare. She conceded, choosing an ear for each family member.

Next, we headed to the pasta aisle. What choices! Should it be spaghetti (thick or thin?), tortellini (cheese or meat?), lasagna (plain or spinach?), bow ties, macaroni? Wait a minute, back up. "Bow ties! That's it, Mommy. We never have these!"

In the check-out line, Tara put all of "her" groceries on the moving belt. I handed her the money to pay the clerk, who smiled at me as she handed Tara the change and the receipt. Tara's eyes lit up. "Now I get to keep the change money since it's from my special dinner, right?" Wrong!

On the way home, we discussed the price of groceries, the many steps involved in getting food to the market, and how each step adds to the final cost.

Once home, Tara pulled her wooden stool up to the counter. She rinsed and trimmed the strawberries and selected a festive bowl for serving them. She then painstakingly shucked the ears of corn. She got out the big corn pot, and we added milk and sugar to the water, just like her grandmother taught me.

"This is a lot of work, Mommy, to make dinner, isn't it?"

I smiled, pausing for emphasis, "Yes, darling, it sure is. And Tara, you're doing such a great job! Do you want to set the table next or start the pasta?"

She looked out the kitchen door at her brother, Jake, on the swing set, then looked at me with her big emerald eyes, clearly giving our new plan second thoughts. I told her that dinner was halfway prepared. She looked at me, half pleading. I asked if she'd like me to cook the pasta and set the table for her tonight since this was only her first night making dinner. With a loud "Yes!" she was out the door to join her brother.

Over the next hour, Tara repeated at least twenty times to Jake and me, "I just can't wait for you to taste my dinner. You're going to love it!" When her father came home, she pounced on him, exclaiming, "Daddy! Guess what? I made the dinner tonight. Wait until you taste it!"

Our candlelight dinner that night was a big hit! Tara proudly reviewed for all who would listen the particulars required for its preparation. Jake's barbecue rib dinner the following week turned out just as well, with the small exception of a few shopping cart bruises on my heels and some barbecue-splattered wallpaper that I cleaned after everyone was asleep.

Planning and preparing these meals has given each of my children a needed sense of control and accomplishment regarding mealtime. While preparing dinner takes a bit more time, their enthusiasm makes it worth the effort. Believe it or not, on the nights when I cook alone, I've been hearing things like, "Mom, this sure is a yummy dinner! Thanks! We really appreciate it!"

Slow-Cooked Chicken 'n' Rice

SERVES 4 to 6

When you need a hot, satisfying dinner to be ready to go on the table as soon as you get home from a busy day, this is the way to go!

2 pounds boneless, skinless chicken breasts, cut into 1-inch cubes

2 packages (6 ounces each) wild and long-grain converted rice mix with seasoning packets

2 1/2 cups water

1 can (10 3/4 ounces) condensed broccoli cheese soup

1/2 cup (1 stick) butter, melted

2 medium onions, finely chopped

1 cup broccoli florets (fresh or frozen)

1/2 pound processed cheese spread, cut into 1/2-inch cubes

1 In a 4-quart or larger slow cooker, combine all the ingredients; mix well.

2 Cover and cook on the low setting for 6 to 8 hours.

Timesaving Tip: *If you have a slow cooker stuffed in the back of your cabinet, get it out and dust it off. If you need a new one, you'll be amazed at all the fashionable, improved styles available on the market today at very reasonable prices. Believe me, slow cookers can be your timesaving hero!*

Stovetop Tuna Casserole

Tuna isn't just for sandwiches! It's a great option for a change-of-pace dinner . . . and it's fast too!

SERVES
6 to 8

1 In a soup pot, cook the pasta according to the package directions; drain and return to the pot.

2 Add the soup, tuna, milk, and pepper; mix well. Cook over medium-high heat for 2 to 3 minutes, or until heated through.

3 Sprinkle with the crushed potato chips, and serve.

Timesaving Tip: *Casseroles are great one-dish meals—especially when we need to rely on kitchen staples from our pantry. And if you have time, you can put them together the night before and just bake 'em at dinner time. If you don't have time for that, stovetop versions like this one are the way to go!*

1 pound ziti pasta

2 cans (10 ¾ ounces each) condensed Cheddar cheese soup

2 cans (12 ounces each) tuna, drained and flaked

1 cup milk

½ teaspoon black pepper

1 package (6 ounces) potato chips, crushed

Healthy Hint:

For extra color, crunch and nutrition, add some thawed and drained frozen peas and some drained canned sliced water chestnuts. And go ahead and use baked potato chips instead of fried.

Lemonade Poached Salmon

SERVES 4

If you haven't tried poaching your salmon, it's time you did. Poaching means that food is cooked gently in liquid that is just below the boiling point. It gives food a delicate flavor, generally without adding any fat.

1 cup mayonnaise

1 can (12 ounces) frozen lemonade concentrate, thawed, divided

$1/4$ teaspoon black pepper

$1/4$ cup water

4 salmon fillets (about $1 1/2$ pounds total)

1. In a small bowl, combine the mayonnaise, 3 tablespoons lemonade concentrate, and the pepper; mix well then cover and chill.

2. In a large skillet, combine the remaining lemonade concentrate and the water; bring to a boil over medium-low heat. Add the salmon and reduce the heat to low; cover, and cook for 8 to 10 minutes, or until the fish flakes easily with a fork.

3. Allow the salmon to cool to room temperature and serve with the chilled lemonade sauce.

Healthy Hint:

Few foods are as good for us as salmon. Even though it is considered a fatty fish, it is an excellent source of omega-3 fatty acids, which promote cardiovascular health. Salmon is also packed with protein and virtually devoid of carbohydrates. When we make it with a healthy cooking method like poaching, we can't beat its nutritious goodness!

Serving Tip: *This salmon can also be made in advance and served well chilled for a refreshing light lunch. To give it extra color and flair, garnish each with a sprig of fresh dill and a slice of lemon.*

106

MY CULINARY

Epiphany

BY LINDA APPLE

*T*here are many important "firsts" in life—first step, first word, first kiss and first turkey—the Thanksgiving kind.

My husband, Neal, and I always went over to my parents' for Thanksgiving. We brought the green-bean casserole and the kids; Mom did everything else. But the holiday cooking mantle was passed along to me when we were transferred to another city.

Mom's face had a rosy glow while preparing for Thanksgiving—from enthusiasm, I supposed. She didn't seem to mind cooking such an extensive meal. Why should I? Plus, she wrote clear, step-by-step instructions for me to follow. A cinch.

Thanksgiving week finally arrived and I pulled out my instructions. First, I had to find the "perfect turkey"—one that would feed us and our five children, plus provide ample leftovers for any fascinating dish I could dream up. I bought a twenty-eight pounder.

Next on the "to do" list—thaw him. Naively, I thought that would only take a few hours on the counter, till my husband nixed that plan and told me it would take a week to defrost a bird that big in the refrigerator. I panicked. Thanksgiving was in two days. I needed a quick defrost method. Neal suggested his granny's technique of putting the turkey in the tub and filling it with cold water.

Later that afternoon, we heard strange noises coming from the bathroom. *Thud, splash, thud.* Neal and I ran to the bathroom and found a diaper floating on the flooded floor. Alarmed, I shoved back the shower curtain to find our two-year-old son laying on top of the turkey, pushing himself from one end of the tub to the other, like a bucking bird rodeo. I grabbed him off the main course, and the rest of the day and into the night, I chopped, diced, sliced, mixed, rolled, sautéed, simmered, boiled and baked. I realized something: Mom's rosy glow wasn't because of the enthusiasm. It was heat exhaustion.

The alarm was unusually loud at 5 A.M. Thanksgiving morning. I crawled out of bed and felt my way down the hall to the bathroom to get the turkey out of the tub. In my sleep-deprived stupor, I hoisted him on my hip. Glacier water spilled down my nylon gown, making it cling like a second skin, setting every nerve in my body on red alert. I won't repeat the words I silently screamed.

After peeling off the wrappers, I stared, shocked by the sight of a naked turkey. The only ones I'd ever seen before wore a nice, crispy, brown skin. This cold, clammy thing was pale and pimply. Everything inside me revolted. Glancing at the recipe, it called for the giblets to be removed from the cavity. Only one problem, I couldn't get the stupid legs apart. Some kind of bar held them together. I tugged, yanked and jerked, for fifteen minutes. Finally, the dark, greasy, cavern yawned open—and I was supposed to put my hand in that? After stuffing onions and celery in the carcass and heaving that monster into the oven, I slammed the door shut and leaned against it. This wasn't the way I remembered Thanksgiving at all.

Later that morning, the savory aroma and lively music I remembered from childhood filled the house. The kids were piled on their daddy watching the Macy's Thanksgiving Day Parade while I feverishly worked in the kitchen wearing that blasted rosy glow.

Finally, dinner was served. My husband said grace, and in less than twenty minutes we consumed one-hundred dollars worth of food that took two days to prepare. After dinner, Neal reclined in his chair, and the kids ran outside. I was left in a kitchen that looked like Bourbon Street the morning after Mardi Gras. So this is what my mother did every year? My hands were chapped. My fingers were cut and burned. Every muscle in my body begged for a glass of wine and a hot bubble bath. As far as I was concerned, my mom deserved sainthood.

Glancing out the window, I watched the children jump into a pile of leaves, just like I did when I was a child. My husband snored in his easy chair, just like Dad. And I began the arduous task of cleaning, just like Mom. Indulging in a little self pity, I grumbled under my breath. Nobody had a clue how hard it was cooking Thanksgiving dinner. Come to think of it, neither did I till now. Getting off my self-righteous perch, I practiced the true meaning of Thanksgiving. I called my mother and said, "Thank you for all your hard work. We are not worthy of you!"

Restaurant-Style Shrimp Scampi

SERVES 4 to 6

You might expect to pay quite a bit for shrimp scampi at a nice restaurant. But look how simple it is to make this lighter version at home (and you get to keep some of that savings in your wallet).

1 pound uncooked linguine

2 tablespoons olive oil

1 pound medium shrimp, peeled and deveined, with tails left on

12 garlic cloves, crushed

1 teaspoon salt

$\frac{1}{2}$ teaspoon black pepper

$\frac{1}{2}$ cup dry white wine

2 tablespoons chopped fresh parsley

1. Cook the linguine according to the package directions; drain, rinse, drain again, and cover to keep warm.

2. Meanwhile, in a large skillet, heat the oil over medium-high heat. Add the shrimp, garlic, salt, and pepper, and sauté for 2 to 3 minutes, until the shrimp turn pink and are cooked through.

3. Reduce the heat to low and add the wine and parsley to the skillet; simmer for 1 to 2 minutes. Toss the shrimp with the linguine. Serve immediately.

Serving Tip: *Give the shrimp a squeeze of fresh lemon right before tossing with the pasta. Mmm mmm!*

Healthy Hint:

For even more heartiness and nutrition, use whole-wheat or spinach linguine.

110

Creamy Scallops

Scallops are versatile because they can be sautéed, grilled, broiled or even poached, and they can be added to soups, stews and salads. What makes them even more appealing is that they cook really fast . . . and that's what we're always looking for, aren't we?

SERVES 4 to 6

1. Preheat the oven to 450°F.

2. Place the scallops in an 8-inch square baking dish; sprinkle with mushrooms.

3. In a medium bowl, combine the soup, heavy cream, wine, salt, and pepper; mix well. Pour over the scallops and mushrooms; sprinkle with the bread crumbs.

4. Bake for 25 to 30 minutes, or until bubbling and the scallops are cooked through.

Did You Know . . . *that this meaty seafood is high in protein? It's found in two general varieties: bay and sea scallops. Since the meat of bay scallops is sweeter than sea scallops, and they're less plentiful, they're usually more expensive. Sea scallops (which I call for here) are more widely available and, though they're larger and generally a bit chewier than bay scallops, their meat is still moist and sweet. Frozen scallops can be found year 'round, and they will work just fine in here too.*

1 1/2 pounds sea scallops

1/2 pound fresh sliced mushrooms

1 can (10 3/4 ounces) condensed cream of celery soup

1/2 cup heavy cream

1/4 cup dry white wine

1/2 teaspoon salt

1/4 teaspoon black pepper

2 tablespoons Italian bread crumbs

Lasagna Roll-Ups

SERVES 4 to 6

Making lasagna into separate rolls means it's really easy to portion and serve, so try it for your next potluck dinner.

1 jar (28 ounces) spaghetti sauce

12 to 14 lasagna noodles, cooked according to the package instructions and drained (see Tip)

1 cup (4 ounces) shredded part-skim mozzarella cheese

Filling

1 container (2 pounds) part-skim ricotta cheese

1 cup (4 ounces) shredded part-skim mozzarella cheese

$1/3$ cup grated Parmesan cheese

3 eggs, beaten

1 tablespoon chopped fresh parsley

1 teaspoon salt

1. Preheat the oven to 375°F. Coat a 9" x 13" baking dish with nonstick cooking spray and pour half the spaghetti sauce over the bottom of the dish.

2. In a large bowl, combine the filling ingredients; mix well. Lay the lasagna noodles out flat and spread the filling evenly over each. Roll up the noodles tightly, and arrange seam-side down in the baking dish. Pour the remaining sauce over the roll-ups, and sprinkle with the remaining 1 cup mozzarella.

3. Bake for 35 to 40 minutes, or until golden and heated through. Let set for 12 to 15 minutes before serving.

Preparation Tip: *A one-pound box of lasagna contains about 20 noodles.*

Healthy Hint:

Add a thawed 10-ounce package of frozen chopped spinach to the filling. (Squeeze the spinach to remove as much liquid as possible.)

Roasted Red Pepper Ravioli

Instead of opening the ordinary jar of red sauce for your ordinary cheese ravioli, throw together this roasted red pepper sauce. In minutes, you can make your own extraordinary sauce that's sure to have everybody thinking you fussed for hours!

SERVES 3 to 4

1. In a large pot, cook the ravioli according to the package directions; drain.

2. Meanwhile, in a food processor or blender, process the peppers, Parmesan cheese, half-and-half, and garlic until smooth.

3. Add the red pepper sauce to the ravioli; toss gently until well coated. Serve immediately.

1 package (24 ounces) frozen cheese ravioli

1 jar (12 ounces) roasted sweet red peppers, drained

1 cup grated Parmesan cheese

½ cup half-and-half

2 garlic cloves

Serving Tip: *Serve with crusty bread and a tossed salad for a quick anytime meal.*

Timesaving Tip: *Frozen pasta and roasted red peppers are on my list of things that you should keep on hand in your freezer and pantry so you always have a quick but interesting dinner option.*

Rigatoni Bolognese

This version of the classic Italian meat sauce tastes like it's been simmering all day and it pairs perfectly with wide rigatoni pasta for a quick dish the whole family will love!

1½ pounds rigatoni

1 pound ground beef

1 carrot, shredded

1 medium onion, diced

1 garlic clove, minced

2 cans (15 ounces each) tomato sauce

1 beef bouillon cube

1 teaspoon sugar

1 teaspoon dried basil

1 teaspoon dried oregano

½ teaspoon Italian seasoning

1 Cook the rigatoni according to the package directions; drain and set aside to keep warm.

2 Meanwhile, in a large pot, brown the beef over medium-high heat. Drain the excess liquid.

3 Add the carrot, onion, and garlic to the beef. Cook for 4 to 5 minutes, or until the onion is tender, stirring occasionally.

4 Add the remaining ingredients except the rigatoni; cover and reduce the heat to low. Simmer for 20 minutes, allowing the flavors to "marry," stirring occasionally. Stir in the cooked rigatoni and serve.

Option: *Sure, this can also be made with ground veal or pork, or a combination of ground meats.*

Garnishing Tip: *Sprinkle on some freshly grated Parmesan cheese just before serving.*

The Latkes Epidemic

BY HARRIET MAY SAVITZ

If I were to explain the making of latkes, it might take me many more words than I can spare. How could one define a mere combination of flour, onion, potato and oil becoming an epidemic that defies all boundaries? Latkes are not just food. They are an experience that is to be shared. A combination of family, friends, and tradition, and a moment to be remembered. Their power can also be overwhelming.

It is a tradition that my daughter makes latkes every Chanukah. We are not certain why they are not made at any other time of year. Certainly, it is a combination of simple ingredients that could be easily purchased any day of the month. Perhaps if we had latkes more often, we might tire of them, and then, come Chanukah, it would not become such an event. Or an epidemic.

It always begins with the decision, how many latkes to cook. The list grows each year. There is the "take-out" order. Those are the latkes promised to neighbors and friends from the year before.

"Remember, when you make them, save me some," a friend would request. And so "some" becomes twenty or thirty or forty. There are also the educational latkes. Students from the children's school who do not realize how contagious the epidemic can become request a taste. And so there are thirty more to add to the list.

Then, of course, there are the workers' latkes. Anyone who helps grate the potatoes, slice and chop the onions, or fry the latkes in the oil is also entitled to employee's compensation. They would strike and leave their jobs if they could not eat some latkes. On a yearly basis, workers usually consume about fifty Latkes.

The party latkes cannot be forgotten. Since there are Chanukah parties and Christmas parties, the latkes travel from celebration to celebration. These parties have been known to consume about 200 latkes. But the epidemic spreads even further for the guests who might never have tasted a latke before and are no longer immune.

"Maybe you should bring a few more next year," someone suggests.

The traveling latkes also cannot be ignored. Relatives traveling from different states and different cities to visit during the holiday season are not to be denied. They, too, expect latkes when they arrive during this time of year. So latkes have to go into the freezer. About 100 go there for insurance.

"You didn't eat them up already?" becomes a familiar question, even before suitcases are unpacked.

There is a lot of pressure on the Latkes Maker. This year, my daughter decided to have fewer workers. She thought she would do it quickly, using her family to help. Perhaps make less. After all, who would know? Of course, she did not realize that the epidemic had already begun, and there was no stopping it now.

She forgot that one cannot stifle, enclose or control the aroma of latkes. Once they are in the frying pan, once they begin to sizzle, once the onions take control, everything smells from latkes. The walls. The house. The clothes. And the neighborhood. Who would know? Just about the entire town, if the wind was flowing in the right direction.

"I've got to get some fresh air," my son-in-law announced as the kitchen filled with smoke, for certainly when an epidemic begins, there is an odor that takes the breath away. And thick onion-smoke is part of it. Windows opened, and the latkes epidemic was on its way.

The latkes aroma drifted from house to house. And soon workers were running from their homes toward one destination: the latkes frying pan.

The total sum of latkes completed reached 300. About fifty more were devoured along the way. Everyone in the neighborhood carried their latkes aroma back to their houses with them. It might take a year for all to recover and continue with their normal lives, latkes-free.

Unfortunately, I must report, there is no cure.

Spaghetti Pie

SERVES 6

One of my most requested recipes, this is a different way to enjoy everybody's favorite spaghetti with cheese. I guarantee this one will become a favorite with your family in no time!

½ pound cooked spaghetti

2 tablespoons olive oil *or* melted butter

2 large eggs, well beaten

½ cup plus 2 tablespoons grated Parmesan cheese, divided

1 cup ricotta cheese

1 cup spaghetti sauce

½ cup (2 ounces) shredded mozzarella cheese

1. Preheat the oven to 350°F.

2. In a large bowl, toss the spaghetti with the olive oil. In a small bowl, combine the eggs and ½ cup Parmesan cheese. Stir into the spaghetti then pour into a lightly greased 10-inch pie plate, and form into a "crust."

3. Spread the ricotta evenly over the crust, but not quite to the edge, and top with the spaghetti sauce. Bake uncovered for 25 minutes.

4. Top with the shredded mozzarella, and bake for 5 more minutes, or until the cheese melts. Remove from the oven and sprinkle with the remaining 2 tablespoons Parmesan cheese. Cool for 10 minutes before slicing into wedges.

Timesaving Tip: *This works well made in advance and frozen without cooking. Just thaw then bake when you're ready to serve it.*

118

American Goulash

"Stars and stripes forever" . . . and goulash, too! That's what you'll think once you dig your fork into this American classic.

SERVES
4 to 6

1 Preheat the oven to 350°F. Coat a 2½-quart casserole dish with nonstick cooking spray.

2 In a large skillet, brown the ground beef, bell pepper, and onion over medium-high heat for 6 to 8 minutes, until no pink remains in the beef, stirring frequently. Drain off the excess liquid.

3 Add the remaining ingredients except the cheese; mix well. Place in the casserole dish, cover, and bake for 25 minutes.

4 Remove casserole from the oven and top with mozzarella cheese. Return to the oven and bake, uncovered, for 15 to 20 more minutes, or until thoroughly heated and the cheese has melted.

1½ to 2 pounds ground beef

½ of a medium-sized green bell pepper, chopped

1 small onion, chopped

1 jar (28 ounces) spaghetti sauce

1 tablespoon garlic salt

½ teaspoon black pepper

8 ounces uncooked elbow macaroni

½ cup water

1 cup (4 ounces) shredded mozzarella cheese

Timesaving Tip: *This is a perfect dish to make ahead and freeze. You can even freeze it in individual portions so the kids can microwave a dish of it after school or any time they need a quick meal.*

Traffic Light Pasta

SERVES 4 to 6

Packed with red, yellow and green veggies, this one's a winner! Check out how fresh it looks on the cover.

1 package (12 ounces) bow tie (farfalle) pasta

¾ pound boneless, skinless chicken breast, cut into thin strips

1 bottle (16 ounces) creamy pepper-Parmesan salad dressing

1 cup cherry tomatoes, cut in half

1 medium-sized yellow bell pepper, cut into thin strips

1 package (10 ounces) frozen asparagus spears, thawed and cut in half

1 In a 6-quart soup pot, cook the pasta according to the package directions; drain, rinse, drain again, and set aside in the colander.

2 Add the remaining ingredients to the pot and cook for 10 to 12 minutes over medium-high heat, or until no pink remains in the chicken, stirring frequently.

3 Return the pasta to the pot and toss to coat; cook for 1 to 2 minutes, or until the pasta is heated through. Serve immediately.

Healthy Hint:

This is a great way to introduce new veggies to your family. Use these, or substitute or add other new ones along with family favorites. And you can use regular or whole-wheat pasta to boost the fiber numbers.

120

GO-ALONGS

Wilted Spinach Salad

When we were kids, we needed Popeye to convince us that spinach would make us strong. Now that we're grown up, and we have recipes as yummy as this one, we don't mind eating spinach at all (and we love that we're also getting loads of good-for-us iron and Vitamins A and C)!

SERVES 2 to 3

1. In a large skillet or soup pot, heat the olive oil over medium heat. Add the spinach, garlic, salt, and pepper, and cook for 30 to 45 seconds, stirring occasionally.

2. Remove skillet from the heat, and toss with the sun-dried tomatoes and pine nuts. Serve immediately.

- 2 tablespoons olive oil
- 1 package (9 ounces) fresh spinach
- 2 garlic cloves, minced
- ⅛ teaspoon salt
- ¼ teaspoon black pepper
- ¼ cup chopped oil-packed sun-dried tomatoes
- 1 tablespoon pine nuts, toasted

Timesaving Tip: *Today we're really lucky to be able to pick up tender, fresh spinach that's already washed and trimmed and waiting for us in the supermarket produce department all year 'round. It sure beats the gritty, sand-filled spinach of the old days! Pick up a bag for this warm salad or for a refreshing cold spinach salad.*

Serving Tip: *Serve topped with fresh cracked black pepper.*

123

Tomato Bread Salad

SERVES 4 to 6

This is no ordinary salad of tomatoes, cucumbers and Italian dressing. Oh, no! It's a few steps up from the everyday salad, yet it doesn't take much more effort and it's sure to get you loads of raves.

4 ripe tomatoes, seeded and cut into 1-inch chunks

1/2 cup Italian dressing

3 1/2 cups toasted bread cubes or packaged croutons (see Tip)

1 medium cucumber, seeded and cubed

1/2 of a large red onion, thinly sliced

2 teaspoons Italian seasoning

1/4 teaspoon black pepper

1 package (8 ounces) mixed greens, optional

1. In a large bowl, combine the tomatoes and dressing; mix well and marinate for at least 15 minutes.

2. Stir in the remaining ingredients except the mixed greens; toss and serve as is or over mixed greens.

Preparation Tip: *Making your own toasted bread cubes is a snap. Simply preheat the oven to 375°F. Place the bread cubes in a single layer on a baking sheet and bake for 15 minutes, or until golden, stirring twice. Allow to cool then use as directed.*

The Plate Made the Meal

BY MARYJO FAITH MORGAN

It was a hand-made gift from a dear friend, unexpected and touching. Golden letters danced around the edge of the red ceramic plate proclaiming, "You Are Special Today." We use it for occasions like birthdays or good report cards—whenever we want someone to feel special.

Incredibly pleased at her thoughtfulness, I assured Judy I'd put it to good use. I was afraid if I put it in the cupboard for safekeeping, her careful handwork would go unappreciated and unused. So the very next day, the plate, held by a wire plate hanger, hung in a fitting spot where we'd see it daily.

We found many uses for the special plate. Significant events were celebrated with it, like school projects finished on time and salary increases. If a friend from school came home to dinner, he got to eat off the red plate. When a niece stopped as she traveled across the country, she ate every dinner of her short stay on it. If extended obligations made someone miss dinner, leftover portions sat waiting to welcome them home on the special plate. We took it off the wall so often, a plate rail was installed so we didn't have to fiddle with the wire hanger each time.

There are days as a parent, no matter how we try to be fair, that we lash out unreasonably. Usually it is something else altogether that has us stressed to begin with. Then what might be a small issue suddenly explodes into an all-out argument. One such outburst left me wondering how my son would ever grow up a balanced individual if I couldn't keep my own temper, let alone teach him how to manage his.

126

When it was time for dinner, he found the red plate at his place. The moment he sat down, he gave me an "Aw, it's okay" grin. I liked the way we could express something without words using this plate! I silently vowed to be a more patient parent.

Fast forward a few years. Raging hormones inhabited the house now. The teen years had hit. Discussions grew more heated. Differing opinions and the quest for independence induced shouting and frustration. Intending only to counsel or instruct, I found myself jousting loud contests of will.

After one particularly exhausting session, I was in a quandary. I didn't even want to discuss it. That was it. Even after things were quiet, I stood cooking our evening meal, stymied and disheartened.

When I put dinner on the table, I was still engrossed in my thoughts. Angry epithets persisted just behind my lips, and I struggled to swallow them unspoken. I took my place at the table, but I was miserable, discouraged, indignant. I didn't even want to eat, and I sat with my eyes closed.

I heard motion at my elbow and I assumed I should pass the food. When I opened my eyes, the red plate sat in front of me. My son's face held a mixture of uncertainty and defiance. Rebellion may have vied with reconciliation, but he hadn't thrown down a gauntlet.

Not at all.

He'd waved an olive branch that looked suspiciously like a red plate.

Country Corn Relish

SERVES 6 to 8

When you're looking for a side dish packed with flavor, texture, and eye appeal, this one's the hands-down winner. Give it a try, whether you have fresh corn on hand or use that good ol' pantry staple canned corn.

1/3 cup vegetable oil

1/4 cup cider vinegar

1/4 cup chopped fresh parsley

2 teaspoons sugar

1/2 teaspoon dried basil

1/4 teaspoon crushed red pepper

2 cans (15 1/4 ounces each) whole kernel corn, drained (see Option)

3 scallions, thinly sliced

2 large tomatoes, diced

1 medium-sized green bell pepper, diced

1 In a large bowl, combine the oil, vinegar, parsley, sugar, basil, and crushed red pepper; mix well.

2 Add the remaining ingredients and stir until well combined. Cover and chill for several hours, or overnight, before serving.

Option: Go ahead and substitute 2/3 cup Italian dressing for the oil, vinegar, and basil; and use fresh corn cut off the cob, if you'd like.

Lemon-Roasted Asparagus

When I was a kid, spring was the only time of the year when we'd be able to have fresh asparagus. We're lucky now that we can get it year 'round in our supermarkets. Look for it on your next shopping trip.

SERVES
4

1 Preheat the oven to 400°F. Place the asparagus in a 9" x 13" baking dish.

2 In a small bowl, combine the butter, lemon juice, and 2 teaspoons of the lemon peel; mix well and pour over the asparagus. Bake for 20 to 25 minutes, or until desired tenderness (see Tip).

3 Remove from the oven and sprinkle with the remaining 2 teaspoons lemon peel. Serve immediately.

2 pounds fresh asparagus, trimmed

2 tablespoons butter, melted

4 tablespoons fresh lemon juice

4 teaspoons grated lemon peel, divided

Preparation Tip: *To prepare asparagus, all you have to do is break or cut off the tough ends and rinse the spears. Cooking time will vary depending on the thickness of the asparagus. Very thin asparagus will cook much faster than very thick asparagus. And, of course, everybody likes it cooked to a different degree of doneness, so keep an eye on it.*

Healthy Hint:

Asparagus is packed with nutrients, and is really versatile, since it can be cooked in the microwave, steamed, stir-fried, or roasted, and it takes just minutes to become crisp-tender. It can be enjoyed warm or cold, so be sure to buy it often for preparing alone or adding to other dishes.

THE SECRET INGREDIENT

BY JEAN BRODY

We were in graduate school working on a migrating bird study and, as part of the package, we were given a wonderful log cabin on the University Experimental Farm to live in. As a young wife and mother who was trying to continue her studies, the cabin was a real bonus to me, as was the rural atmosphere of the farm, 100 miles from the bustle of the university. But one of our "fringe jobs" was to entertain anyone the Ecology Department wanted to send to the farm, which would almost always include a meal we would have to prepare. Early on I decided to create an organic vegetable garden on the farm so that most of what I served would be from this non-polluted soil. They thought it was a great idea, and Jean's Garden was born.

One late summer, day we got a call from the university that a very well-known man and his wife would be coming up. In fact, this gentleman was a Nobel Peace Prize recipient, so I wanted to make a special "deal of a meal." Several weeks before, we also were trying to entertain university guests by taking them up to Louisiana, Missouri, to board a riverboat for a scenic ride through the area we were studying. While carrying my baby, I tripped and fell all the way down the steep levee steps leading to the boat. It was a mother-instinct moment. Without even thinking, I tucked him close to my body so that, as I rolled, he never even touched the steps. I, however, was landing on jutted elbows, managing to break my left elbow in a compound fracture.

Our riverboat excursion was aborted, and a trip to the local hospital rendered me with a heavy cast from under my shoulder blade down to my fingertips. A hole had been left for my thumb to protrude, and the cast covered the palm of my left hand. To say this complicated my life is

130

a giant understatement. Even sweeping the old wood-plank floors was a real trick. However, when we were asked to entertain this famous couple, I was determined to make it a perfect meal.

Among the many vegetables I grew were beautiful potatoes, and I wanted to make mashed potatoes as part of the meal. I had help from my little brother Jim in gathering the vegetables, as well as pealing and dicing them, and all was on schedule. We'd set a great long table outside the cabin, and Jim had done a great job of placing plates, napkins and utensils around.

All that was left was mashing the potatoes. The guests were beginning to seat themselves around the table and nibble on my homemade pickles, so I shooed everybody out of the cabin kitchen while I mashed the potatoes in peace. They were piping hot and smelled wondrous. I added milk and lots of real butter and began to mash the mixture. I had an old-fashioned hand beater where you hold the handle in one hand and turned with the other. It so happened that I held it with my left hand, pushing it into my palm, which was covered with the plaster cast.

Feeling a bit flustered by that time, I was turning that rotor like a crazy woman, making the blades burrow deeply into the soft potatoes. All of a sudden, I looked down, and where the handle of the hand beater was pressing into my left palm, a fine, steady mist of plaster-of-paris from my cast was fluttering into the mixture. I froze. How much plaster had gone into the bowl? Is it harmful to digest? And—the most burning question of all—could anybody tell? I mean, potatoes are white and so is plaster, and there were no chunks of it down in there.

Oh, lord help me. In one frantic and irrational split second, I decided to go right ahead and serve that warm bowl of mashed potatoes. I did! They looked especially tasty because they had a little . . . um . . . texture and body to them. Actually, of all the vegetables, the mashed potatoes were the main hit.

As everyone ate, I silently prayed that the potatoes would be eaten before they "set" and that nobody would get sick, which they didn't. As a matter of fact, days later I received a thank-you note from the famous man's wife and, in it, she asked for my recipe for the delicious mashed potatoes. I was happy to share it—leaving out one very secret ingredient.

Roasted Plum Tomatoes

Try this simple side of flavorful, juicy plum tomatoes to add excitement to tonight's dinner. Your gang will surely be checking their calendars to see what the special occasion is!

2 tablespoons vegetable oil

1 teaspoon salt

1/4 teaspoon black pepper

1/4 teaspoon garlic powder

1/4 teaspoon onion powder

12 plum tomatoes

2 tablespoons chopped fresh basil

1. Preheat the oven to 450°F. In a large bowl, combine all the ingredients except the tomatoes and basil.

2. Cut the tomatoes in half lengthwise and gently squeeze out the seeds and juice. Toss in the oil mixture then pour into a 9" x 13" baking dish.

3. Roast for 20 to 25 minutes, or until tender but not overcooked. Sprinkle with the basil, and serve.

Healthy Hint:

Including tomatoes (probably my favorite food) in any meal plan is a smart choice because they're packed with lycopene— a natural compound that gives fruit and veggies their bright colors and supports the immune system. Tomatoes also contain antioxidants, which may provide protection from certain types of cancers. With all that tomatoes have to offer, enjoy their benefits all year long!

Honey-Glazed Carrots

Serve your honeys this honey of a side dish and you're guaranteed to get lots of sweet praise!

SERVES
4

1 Place the carrots in a medium saucepan. Add enough water to cover; bring to a boil over high heat. Reduce the heat to medium-high, cover, and cook for 15 to 20 minutes, or until desired tenderness; drain the carrots well and set aside.

2 In the saucepan, melt the butter over medium heat. Add the remaining ingredients; mix well.

3 Return the carrots to the saucepan and toss until mixed well and heated through. Serve immediately.

Option: *If you'd prefer to use whole carrots for this, slice them diagonally before boiling. I call for baby carrots because it's so simple to just open the bag and go!*

1 pound baby carrots
  (see Option)
2 tablespoons butter
2 tablespoons honey
$\frac{1}{2}$ teaspoon lemon juice
$\frac{1}{2}$ teaspoon ground ginger
$\frac{1}{4}$ teaspoon salt

Healthy Hint:

Carrots are packed with Vitamin A, as well as a type of fiber that is thought to lower blood cholesterol. They're a satisfying snack eaten raw, and they make a hearty addition to stews, soups and other cooked dishes, as well as making a great side dish in their own right, as in this recipe.

133

NOTHING TO SHARE

BY MARYJO FAITH MORGAN

I t hit me during afternoon naptime. The potluck. It's tonight!

I was really looking forward to it. Since I'd begun daily daycare I felt pretty isolated from adult conversation despite my busy toddler and other little ones filling my days.

Besides, potlucks always impress me. There are no assignments. No one makes a list of how many are bringing main entrées, side dishes or desserts. No one figures out how many servings are needed to feed the expected number of guests. There is a huge variety. What might not have made a well-rounded meal at home is a plentiful part of the "larger whole" here. Everyone just brings "something," and like stone soup, an abundance results, filling the air with tantalizing aromas. Everyone politely says nothing about repeated trips back to sample yet another dab of this mouth-watering casserole or that chocolate delight. There is lots of conversation and laughter. Cooking techniques and secrets are readily traded. There is but one rule: share. We all go home content.

I'd planned on taking manicotti. I always took manicotti. It was my specialty. Not many people made homemade Italian food here the way we did where I was raised. I was proud to share my heritage, and my manicotti was a popular dish at any gathering. I was asked for the recipe so often, I took to bringing along a couple copies already written up on index cards.

But when I attempted to assemble the necessary ingredients, I found that my cupboard was bare of the essentials. No ricotta, no mozzarella, no eggs. Sometimes I served manicotti with a side dish of spicy sausage, but today the freezer held only a quarter-pound of bacon, some stew meat and a few frosty vegetable packages smashed way back in the corner. I looked in the "food budget" envelope, but knew there was only enough for bread and milk until payday.

It is not in the spirit of potlucking to arrive with only plates and flatware, so I could not go empty-handed. There would be no potluck for me tonight. No circle of friendly faces smiling over piled-high plates. No enticing smells of other kitchens and family recipes. No, I simply could not go. I wanted to cry.

I knew I had to make dinner anyway, so back to the freezer I returned. I'd thaw the meat, make gravy and turn those bagged veggies into some kind of stew. But . . . all three packages were corn! I threw them back into the freezer and slammed the door. Understand, I had been raised in what local license plates say is the "Garden State." Fresh Jersey corn, succulent, sweet and juicy, is some of the tastiest corn grown anywhere. When we cooked corn at home, we'd figure three or four apiece easy. Corn cut from the cob just didn't have the same appeal to me, frozen corn sounded awful, and what was a stew with only meat and corn?

Before I could go any further with dinner preparations, sounds emitting from the bedroom told me naptime was over. Soon, little ones needing snacks and attention crowded my thoughts.

Corn. Corn? As I washed sticky hands and kissed a boo-boo, I puzzled over it. Ta-da! A side dish from my mother-in-law popped into my mind. Simple . . . delicious and, yes, worthy to share.

It seemed like an odd combination to me, but after my first taste I'd surprised everyone, including myself, by taking seconds. Of all things, a combo of corn and bacon! Carefully, I warmed the frozen bacon to separate the strips. Once browned and drained, I crumbled it, added the corn and a bit of sugar, and allowed the corn to caramelize. Soon the kitchen windows were steamed, and the house smelled wonderful. A tiny dash of salt, some freshly ground pepper, and it was ready.

We all changed and were out the door quickly. The covered dish, wrapped in warm towels, sat on the seat beside me. I was deeply pleased. I did have something to share after all.

When everyone was settled with a plate, I went to fill my own. As I moved through the line, I received compliments on my corn from people who had grown up on farms in Illinois, Iowa or Nebraska—people who had eaten corn in every conceivable configuration. When I got to it, I was surprised to find little left of my corn. I should have known that here in the heartland, corn is a staple, and most folks are eager to try a different twist on an old standby. Good thing I had a few index cards. I suddenly had a new specialty.

Vegetable Stir-Fry

SERVES 8

When you're throwing your main course on the grill or doing something else really simple, put together this crunchy, fresh side dish.

1 can (15 ounces) baby corn, drained and liquid reserved

2 tablespoons light soy sauce

2 tablespoons cornstarch

1 teaspoon crushed red pepper

¼ cup peanut oil

4 garlic cloves, minced

1 bunch broccoli, cut into small florets

2 medium bell peppers (1 red and 1 yellow), cut into ½-inch strips

1 large onion, cut into wedges

½ pound fresh sliced mushrooms

½ pound snow peas, trimmed

1 In a small bowl, combine the reserved liquid from the corn, the soy sauce, cornstarch, and crushed red pepper; set aside.

2 In a large skillet or wok, heat the peanut oil over high heat until hot. Add the garlic, broccoli, peppers, onion, and mushrooms. Stir-fry for 6 to 7 minutes, or until the vegetables are crisp-tender.

3 Add the snow peas and baby corn and stir-fry for 3 to 4 minutes, or until the snow peas turn bright green.

4 Add the soy sauce mixture, and stir-fry for 1 to 2 minutes, or until the sauce thickens. Serve immediately.

Healthy Hint:

Researchers say green veggies in a low-fat diet help our vision, strengthen bones and teeth, and can contribute to lowering cancer risks. *Now* will you eat your veggies?

Veggie-Lover's Delight

SERVES 5

This fresh dish goes with just about everything, and it's a great way to enjoy the tastes of summer any time of year!

1 package (6 ounces) baby carrots

3 tablespoons butter

3 zucchini, cut into 1-inch chunks

3 yellow squash, cut into 1-inch chunks

1 tablespoon chopped fresh dill weed

1/4 teaspoon onion powder

1/2 teaspoon salt

1/2 teaspoon black pepper

1 Place the carrots in a medium saucepan and add just enough water to cover them. Bring to a boil over medium-high heat and cook for 8 to 10 minutes, or until fork-tender; drain.

2 In a large skillet, melt the butter over medium heat and add the carrots and remaining ingredients; stir until well combined. Cook for 6 to 8 minutes, or until the vegetables are tender.

Garnishing Tip: *To give this extra flair, top with a sprig of dill weed just before serving.*

Herb-Roasted Corn on the Cob

No matter if you roast this in the oven or on the grill, it's a new way to jazz up an old favorite while adding fiber to your diet. One taste and you'll never put plain butter on your ears again.

SERVES 4

1. Preheat the oven to 425°F. In a small bowl, combine all the ingredients except the corn; mix well.

2. Place each ear of corn in a separate piece of aluminum foil and brush with the butter mixture. Wrap each and seal completely then place on a rimmed baking sheet.

3. Roast the corn for 20 to 25 minutes, or until the kernels are tender. Carefully open the foil and remove the corn. Serve immediately.

2 tablespoons butter, melted

1 garlic clove, minced

1 scallion, finely chopped

1 teaspoon chopped fresh dill weed

$\frac{1}{8}$ teaspoon black pepper

4 ears fresh corn on the cob, husked

Did You Know . . . *that we can enjoy fresh corn practically all year long in any part of the country? Yup, we can, thanks to Supersweet corn from Florida. This is not just any corn! It's even sweeter than the corn that used to be only available locally in the summertime and only sweet on the day it was picked. The result of years of research and development, this corn's sweet flavor and terrific color will last for about a week after harvesting. We can enjoy this recipe any time of the year!*

139

WHERE'S THE TURKEY?

BY BARBARA LOMONACO

I t was Thanksgiving Day—my most favorite holiday of the year. We had invited a house full of people over, both family and friends, for our traditional dinner, and I had ordered a huge turkey so there would be enough for dinner that night and plenty of leftovers for the next day. Dinner was planned for six o'clock, so I had to get the turkey in the oven by ten in the morning.

It was a family tradition that all of us, my husband and my three sons, shared the work of getting the turkey ready. First, we made the stuffing. Then we had to have a taste test to be sure that it was just right. We always made more stuffing than we could ever use because it seemed we always tasted more than we ever needed to! The boys took turns packing the stuffing in the bird, and then they rubbed the turkey with olive oil. My husband sewed the turkey closed so that the stuffing couldn't escape while I seasoned the bird. Soon, it was ready to roast. This year it was so big that it almost didn't fit into the oven, but, after some maneuvering, in it went. We set the oven at 325 degrees and the timer for eight hours.

People started arriving mid-afternoon, and the wonderful aroma of the turkey filled the house and floated out to the front porch. We all knew that this was going to be one of the best turkeys we had ever had. Every so often, we basted the turkey until it was golden brown and looked just delicious. It was a beautiful bird. We couldn't wait to eat.

All of our guests brought a side dish to go along with the turkey. We

140

had lots of appetizers, a wonderful cream of potato leek soup, rolls, a delicious salad with shrimp, three kinds of vegetables, stuffing, mashed potatoes, yams, cranberries—both homemade and store-bought—and desserts, desserts, desserts. We had enough food to feed a small nation!

At last, it was time to eat. All twenty-five of us sat down to begin our holiday meal. I served the soup with a silver ladle my grandmother had brought with her when she came to this country. It is very precious to me, and I think that using that ladle makes the soup taste better. Then we had our salad.

Finally, my husband excused himself and headed to the kitchen to begin the carving ceremony. Suddenly, he reappeared at the door to the dining room and asked me to come into the kitchen. It seemed to him that the turkey was still pretty raw inside. How could that be? The bird had been cooking for eight hours already, but he was right. So we turned the oven up to 500 degrees and told everyone at the table to just relax for a while.

After about an hour, we checked the turkey. Still not ready. We removed the stuffing, hoping that it would cook faster. It didn't. It was still raw inside, and it was getting later and later. Finally, we did the only thing that we could do—we decided to just serve all of the delicious dishes that our guests had brought to accompany the bird. While we ate and ate, that tough bird just kept roasting and roasting. The aroma of the turkey was the only turkey we had for dinner that Thanksgiving. And what a terrific meal it was. Everyone decided it was one of the best Thanksgiving dinners we had ever had.

That turkey never completely cooked, and we never were able to figure out why, but it really didn't matter. The food that everyone brought—all of the side dishes to go along with the turkey—fed us well. No one left our house hungry that night; we all had plenty to eat and, most importantly, we were all together—family and friends.

Sautéed Green Beans

SERVES 8

The "5 A Day for Better Health" program recommends that we "go green every day" by including green veggies and fruit in our daily diets. Green vegetables are believed to have significant antioxidant, health-promoting benefits, so get started tonight with these spectacular green beans.

2 tablespoons olive oil

¼ cup slivered almonds

1 garlic clove, minced

2 packages (9 ounces each) frozen French-cut green beans

¼ cup sun-dried tomatoes, chopped

¼ teaspoon salt

¼ teaspoon black pepper

1 In a large skillet, heat the oil over medium heat. Add the almonds and garlic and sauté for 2 to 3 minutes, or until the almonds are light golden.

2 Add the remaining ingredients, cover, and allow the beans to steam for 10 minutes or until tender, stirring occasionally. Serve immediately.

Serving Tip: *These are great as is, or topped with freshly grated Parmesan cheese.*

Healthy Hint:

Canola oil and olive oil both earn a "thumbs up" because they contain monounsaturated fat. This fat fights cholesterol buildup by raising HDL (good) cholesterol levels, so look for it in the products you buy. And just because the label on a particular oil or other product claims that it's "light," be aware that that word may simply be referring to its lighter taste.

142

Classic Mashed Potatoes

This is the classic recipe that everybody loves . . . but since we're always looking for interesting ways to change up our dinner menus, check out my other suggestions for making these into the unexpected treat on your family's dinner plates. Give 'em a try plain or in any of these variations . . . or create your own!

SERVES 6 to 8

1 Place the potatoes in a large soup pot and add just enough water to cover. Bring to a boil over high heat and cook for 12 to 15 minutes, or until tender; drain well and place in a large bowl.

2 Add the remaining ingredients and beat with an electric mixer until smooth and creamy. Serve immediately.

5 pounds potatoes, peeled, sliced $\frac{1}{4}$-inch thick

$\frac{1}{2}$ cup (1 stick) butter, softened

$\frac{3}{4}$ cup milk

2 teaspoons salt

1 teaspoon black pepper

VARIATIONS:

Garlic Smashed Potatoes:

Quarter a small onion and add it, along with 10 peeled, whole garlic cloves, to the pot with the potatoes before bringing them to a boil. Beat as directed above.

Ruby Mashed Potatoes:

Prepare Classic Mashed Potatoes, reducing the milk to $\frac{1}{4}$ cup. Add two well-drained 15-ounce cans of sliced beets. Beat as directed above.

Spinach Mashed Potatoes:

Prepare Classic Mashed Potatoes and add two 10-ounce packages of frozen chopped spinach that have been thawed, drained, and squeezed dry. Beat as directed above. (see photo page 87)

143

Double-Stuffed Potatoes

SERVES
6

These might be a little extra work, but they're definitely worth the effort when you want to serve something special.

6 medium potatoes

½ teaspoon salt

¼ teaspoon pepper

¼ cup sour cream

3 tablespoons butter or margarine

¼ teaspoon onion powder

Paprika for sprinkling

1 Preheat the oven to 400°F.

2 Scrub the potatoes and pierce the skins with a fork. Bake for 55 minutes, or until tender.

3 Slice 1 inch off the top of each potato and scoop out the pulp; place pulp in a medium bowl.

4 Add the salt, pepper, sour cream, butter, and onion powder, and beat with an electric mixer until well combined.

5 Spoon mixture back into the potato shells and lightly sprinkle the tops with paprika.

6 Bake for 30 minutes, or until the potatoes start to brown on top.

Garnishing Tip: *To make these "loaded" double-stuffers, top them with a bit of shredded Cheddar cheese and some bacon bits and scallion rings. Mmm!*

Timesaving Tip: *These can be prepared and frozen for up to one month before baking, if wrapped well. Just thaw in the refrigerator overnight and bake as directed.*

Pantry Panache

BY CAROL MCADOO REHME

"Well, Mother, your trademark dish is still a success," I complimented into the phone.

"What dish is that, dear?"

"Redhot Applesauce, of course. I made it all through the kids' growing-up years and now they're making it, too," I boasted.

"I still don't know what you're talking about." Mother's impatience was obvious. Didn't know what I was talking about? Why, I called the recipe Old Reliable—the people-pleasing, go-with-everything, quick-as-a-wink concoction we toted to every church social. My four kids had expected me to produce it for picnics, potlucks, and holidays during their growing-up years. Besides being a family favorite and a quick meal-stretching side dish, the ingredients were as close as the pantry, nearly always on hand. "Oh, you know," my voice was brisk, "a jar of applesauce with a sprinkling of cinnamon-flavored candies stirred in."

"Uh, I don't believe I . . ."

"Good grief, Mother," I interrupted, "Redhot Applesauce. I've been fixing it for thirty-five years. And I just thought it would impress you to know that now your grandchildren are serving it to their kids and guests. I remember you making it during my childhood and now it's a multi-generational tradition. Why it's practically . . ."

"It's not . . ." she interrupted.

". . . a legacy!" I finished in triumph. "How can you not remember?"

There was a long silence. A big sigh. A grunt. "Tradition? Why, it's not even a real recipe. If my memory serves me right," her grin was nearly audible, "I only made it once—out of desperation. Extra company showed up, and I wanted to stretch the menu so I threw together what I had on hand."

"Canned applesauce and redhots!" I hooted into the phone.

Necessity and inspiration, we laughingly acknowledged, were the only ingredients necessary for a legacy recipe.

Portobello Stuffing

What can't you do with this versatile superstar of mushrooms? Teaming it with bell pepper, onion, sage, and a healthy corn muffin gets you this incredible stuffing with a meaty taste.

SERVES
6

1 In a large skillet, melt the butter over medium-high heat. Add the bell pepper and onion and sauté for 2 to 3 minutes, or until tender.

2 Stir in the mushrooms, sage, and black pepper, and sauté for 3 to 5 minutes, or until the mushrooms are tender.

3 Stir in the crumbled muffin and cook for 2 to 3 more minutes, or until heated through.

2 tablespoons butter

1 medium-sized bell pepper, finely chopped

1 small onion, finely chopped

6 ounces Portobello mushrooms, chopped

2 teaspoons rubbed sage

$1/4$ teaspoon black pepper

1 small corn muffin, crumbled

Healthy Hint:

When you're looking for a hearty option to regular hamburgers, try grilling Portobello mushrooms. Just brush them with a mixture of olive oil and seasonings then grill and serve them as you would beef burgers. Portobellos seem to be made to absorb whatever seasonings you team them with, as you'll find when you make this recipe.

Festive Pilaf

SERVES
8

Pilaf is a dish that has always seemed fancy—maybe it's the combination of colors and textures. Well, whatever it is, trot this one out when you want to say, "You're special."

1 tablespoon butter

1 cup uncooked long- *or* whole-grain rice, divided

2 chicken bouillon cubes

2 cups water

3 scallions, sliced

1/2 of a medium-sized red bell pepper, finely chopped

1/8 teaspoon black pepper

1 In a large skillet, melt the butter over high heat. Brown 1/2 cup rice in the butter, stirring constantly.

2 Add the remaining 1/2 cup rice, the bouillon cubes, and water, and bring to a boil. Reduce the heat to medium-low, cover, and simmer for 18 to 20 minutes.

3 Stir in the scallions, and the red and black peppers, and cook until heated through.

Garnishing Tip: *Top off this tasty go-along with a few scallion rings to give it a festive look.*

Chocolate-Laced Fruit Kabobs

Mention you're serving Chocolate-Laced Fruit Kabobs and get ready to handle the crowds . . . and the compliments!

MAKES
10
KABOBS

1. Cut the cantaloupe half into 5 wedges. Remove the rind and cut each wedge into 4 chunks. Repeat with the honeydew. Cut the pineapple half into 4 wedges. Remove the core and rind then cut each wedge into 5 chunks.

2. On each of the skewers, alternate a strawberry, honeydew chunk, cantaloupe chunk, and pineapple chunk. Repeat so that 8 pieces of fruit are on each skewer. Repeat the entire process so that all 10 skewers are complete. Place them on a waxed paper-covered cookie sheet.

3. In a small saucepan, combine the chocolate chips, butter, and corn syrup over low heat; stir until the chips are melted. Drizzle about ¾ tablespoon chocolate mixture over each fruit skewer.

4. Allow 5 minutes for the chocolate to firm up before serving, or cover and refrigerate until ready to serve.

- ½ of a large cantaloupe
- ½ of a large honeydew melon
- ½ of a large pineapple
- 20 medium-sized strawberries, hulled and cleaned
- 10 wooden or metal skewers (each 10 to 12 inches long)
- ½ cup semisweet chocolate chips
- 1 tablespoon butter
- 2 tablespoons light corn syrup

Healthy Hint:

Make the skewers without the chocolate drizzle for an even healthier snack or a colorful, edible garnish.

Peanut Butter and Jelly Bars

MAKES 15 to 18 BARS

Peanut butter and jelly is a classic combination, so these bars are sure to have your whole gang jumping for joy!

2¼ cups all-purpose flour

½ cup (1 stick) butter, melted

½ cup creamy peanut butter

½ cup packed light brown sugar

¼ cup granulated sugar

1 egg

1 cup strawberry jelly (see Option)

1 Preheat the oven to 350°F. Coat a 9" x 13" baking dish with nonstick cooking spray.

2 In a large bowl, combine all the ingredients except the jelly. Beat with an electric beater on medium speed for 2 minutes, or until blended and crumbly. Reserve 1 cup of the peanut butter mixture and set aside.

3 Spread the remaining mixture over the bottom of the baking dish. Spread the jelly evenly over the mixture and crumble the reserved peanut butter mixture over the top.

4 Bake for 40 to 45 minutes, or until the topping is golden. Allow to cool completely then cut into bars and serve.

Option: *Sure, you can use your favorite flavor of jam or preserves in place of the strawberry jelly.*

My Trusted, Crusty Friend

BY ANNE HOMAN

*T*wenty-five years ago, my many valued possessions included my gleaming copper pots and pans, a state-of-the-art food processor and intricately detailed fine bone china with service for twelve. All were wedding presents, symbols of the domestic skills I hoped I would soon master as a young bride. Early in those twenty-five years, however, I learned I wasn't programmed with an aptitude for cooking. Fortunately, my husband John assumed this role and he is currently breaking in a third set of pots and pans. The food processor died of old age a decade ago and I believe the china is in storage. John likes to serve our meals, instead, on oversized black-rimmed pottery with two loons floating blissfully together on a tranquil lake located in the center of our dinner plates.

Surprisingly, twenty-five years later, I can count my valued possessions on one hand. Among them is a crusty, dog-eared copy of *Better Homes and Gardens Homemade Cookies Cook Book* that I also received for a wedding gift. Unlike my fine bone china, it is irreplaceable. No, I never mastered the culinary secrets of lumpless gravy or leatherless pot roast, but I relied on this book to hone a skill that I knew would come in handy many times: baking cookies so delectable that no mini-mortal could resist them.

As a young mother, I quickly realized that cookies were a remarkable bartering tool for the completion of unpleasant chores, from picking up the playroom to sweeping the walk. "Go help your father clean the garage while I make a batch of cookies," was a suggestion that seldom brought protest. My peanut butter blossoms empowered me as an authority figure. My snickerdoodles brought me celebrity status among many seasons of pint-sized soccer and baseball stars. My oatmeal raisin cookies mended bruised egos and helped cheer disheartened hearts. Even in the stormy years of adolescence, my cookies were the peacekeeper when my son was at odds with his father or my daughter took issue with me. A nonverbal truce was called as soon as the familiar sweet

154

aroma wafted into their corner of the house. The three of them gathered around the island countertop as the cookies were scooped off the baking pan with a spatula and slid onto a sheet of wax paper to cool. It never failed. My cookies were a secret weapon. They brought polar opposites together and, for a few moments, no words were spoken in anger. There was only the sound of sloshing milk and small talk as one hand, then another, reached for a second cookie and a third.

I baked cookies every week—winter, spring, summer and fall. I baked cookies through four presidents' terms of office—Reagan, Bush, Clinton and Bush, Jr. My cookies were a companion to every growing stage from alphabet flashcards to high-school geometry, from Teaching Little Fingers to Play to the theme from Titanic, from Sesame Street to Seinfeld. And, cookie-making time was an open invitation for talking about baseball cards and dying pets, eight-year old crushes and sixteen-year-old love affairs and all of the little insignificant topics in between that bond mothers and children long after they leave home for lives of their own.

When my youngest left for college, it was often hard to turn through the pages of the cookie book, partly because of a corn syrup accident years ago, but mostly because it brought unbearable sadness. Where was the little blonde-haired girl with the stubborn cowlick who crawled up on the stool beside me and read me a recipe, even though I usually had it committed to heart? Where was the ten-year-old boy who wanted me to drill him on the state capitals while I rolled dough into balls and arranged them on the aluminum pan?

Now, I take much better care of my cookie book than I ever did before. It's no longer tossed with the phone book and the water bill on the kitchen desk. And when I get word that our son or daughter is coming home to visit, out it comes, with its yellowed pages and penciled in calculations for doubling or tripling one recipe or another. Although imperceptible to the eye, some of my happiest moments as a mother are documented in the pages of this book, and its value only increases the older I grow.

Half-Moon Cookies

MAKES 1½ DOZEN

Don't wait 'til the next full moon to impress everybody with this bakery favorite straight from your own kitchen!

1 package (18¼ ounces) white cake mix (see Option)

⅔ cup vegetable oil

2 eggs

8 ounces (half a 16-ounce container) chocolate frosting

8 ounces (half a 16-ounce container) vanilla frosting

1 Preheat the oven to 350°F. Coat two cookie sheets with nonstick cooking spray.

2 In a large bowl, combine the cake mix, oil, and eggs; mix well. Drop by heaping tablespoonfuls 2 inches apart onto the cookie sheets. Bake for 12 to 14 minutes, or until firm.

3 Remove the cookies to wire racks to cool completely. Frost half of the flat side of each cookie with vanilla frosting and the other half with chocolate frosting. Serve, or cover loosely until ready to serve.

Option: *To make chocolate half-moon cookies, simply use chocolate cake mix instead of white.*

156

Polka Dot Cookies

If you want to be the hit of the next bake sale, here's your answer! These little cuties look like reverse chocolate chip cookies, and boy, do the kids love 'em!

MAKES 3 to 4 DOZEN

1. Preheat the oven to 350°F. Coat cookie sheets with nonstick cooking spray.

2. In a large bowl, combine the cake mix, oil, and eggs; beat with an electric beater until well blended.

3. With a spoon, stir in the white chocolate chips. Drop by teaspoonfuls 2 inches apart onto the cookie sheets.

4. Bake for 9 to 11 minutes, or until the cookies are firm. Remove the cookies to a wire rack to cool completely.

1 package (18½ ounces) devil's food cake mix
⅓ cup vegetable oil
2 eggs
2 cups (12 ounces) white chocolate chips

Option: *Use this same recipe to make Gumdrop Cookies. Simply substitute yellow cake mix for the devil's food, and 1 cup coarsely chopped gumdrops for the chocolate chips, and maybe bake a few minutes longer . . . or mix and match your other favorite cakes and candies to come up with your own creations!*

157

Chocolate Almond Caramel Apples

MAKES 4 APPLES

Why pay exorbitant amounts of money to buy these for special gifts when you can make 'em yourself for a fraction of the cost? You can customize them and give gifts that are gooey outside and crunchy inside . . . and sure to be enjoyed!

4 large Red Delicious apples, washed and dried

4 wooden craft sticks

1 package (14 ounces) vanilla caramels, unwrapped

2 tablespoons water

1 cup semisweet chocolate chips

$\frac{1}{2}$ cup slivered almonds, toasted

1. Line a large rimmed baking sheet with waxed paper and coat with nonstick cooking spray. Insert the sticks into the stem end of each apple.

2. In a medium saucepan, combine the caramels and water over low heat until melted, stirring constantly. Remove from the heat and spoon over the apples, coating completely. Place the coated apples on the baking sheet and chill for 1 hour.

3. In another medium saucepan, melt the chocolate chips over low heat, stirring constantly. Drizzle the melted chocolate over the caramel apples and sprinkle with the nuts. Return the apples to the baking sheet and chill for 30 minutes, or until set.

Option: *Make these caramel apples your own by covering with your favorite type of chocolate like white, milk, or semisweet, or even using more than one type. And sprinkle with your favorite nuts, sprinkles, or crushed candy.*

Without A Tail

BY MAUREEN JOHNSON

"You're not going to preschool today, Paddy." I announced, between sneezes, to my surprised son. "Why?"

"Because Mommy is staying at home." "Why?"

"Because she's sick." "Why?"

"Because she isn't feeling so good." Annoying questions. "What are we going to do, Mommy?" he asked. "Well, I thought you and I might bake cookies." He looked doubtful. "But you never bake cookies. Grandma and I bake cookies." My head thumped. "Yes, but Grandma doesn't have these animal cookie molds." I flourished the colored plastic.

"That's because Grandma gave them to you, Mommy." Yes, she had. And what more could a working mom ask for on her birthday? I'd spent the last eighteen months trying to figure out if they could be used for massage purposes instead.

"Come up here and help me. We'll make a whole zoo," I told him, tickling him as I lifted him onto the stool. Soon, I had the recipe book primed. I would have been lost without it. I was a reasonably good cook, but baking was not my forte.

"Now help Mommy put the flour into this bowl," I told Paddy.

"Where's your net thing, Mommy?" I paused mid-pour. "Grandma always uses a net." "Why?"

"To stop the balls." "What balls?"

"The ones that live in the flour." Suddenly I understood. I rummaged around in the cupboard until I found the "net thing." Starting again, I began to sieve the flour. "That's the wrong bowl, Mommy." I halted.

"Grandma always uses her cookie bowl for cookies."

"Why?"

"Because it's big." Perhaps he was right. The soup bowl was small. He waited patiently while I found a bigger bowl. "Now you can pour in some sugar," I told him, handing him the heaped spoon. "That's not cookie sugar, Mommy." My head was pounding again. "Why not?"

"Grandma's cookie sugar is brown."

"Mommy's is white," I reassured him. Doubtfully, he poured in half a spoon. "Now I'm going to crack the egg," I said, tapping it on the side of the bowl. His eyes widened. "No! You can't!"

"Why not?"

"Grandma always cracks it into a dish first."

"Why?" "So we can pick out the shells, silly. You don't want shell cookies, Mommy." He giggled. I placed another dish on the bench in dismay. At this rate I'd be cleaning up all morning, and my strength was fading fast. When the egg was in, I mustered up just enough energy to beat the mixture.

"Let's get these cookies in the molds." I handed him the animals, and he carefully set them out on the tray. While the mixture was baking, I cleared away the mess and flopped onto the sofa. Paddy crawled into my lap. I held him and closed my eyes. "Mommy?"

"Mmm?"

"I really want a brother."

"But you have Merlin. He's your brother."

"But Merlin's a dog, Mommy. When am I going to get a brother without a tail?"

Saved by the oven bell.

"Yeah! Cookies!" he yelled, forgetting the brother as we rushed to take them out. I watched nervously as he tasted the first one. "Yummy!" He rubbed his stomach theatrically. I was absurdly relieved as he snatched a second cookie and disappeared. I packed away the leftovers, and I thought about my morning. I'd had a great time baking cookies with my son. Except for the mess and the constant reproaches and my thumping headache, I wouldn't have missed it for the world!

"Mommy," Paddy said, coming back into the kitchen.

"Yeah?" I noticed with satisfaction that both his cookies had been scoffed. "I'm glad I have a brother with a tail."

"Really? I'm pleased to hear that, Paddy. Why?"

"Because a real brother might only like Grandma's cookies, too, and then you wouldn't have anyone to eat yours."

Peanutty M&M® Bars

MAKES 9 to 12 BARS

When those good report cards come home, we want to make a little something special to reward the kids for their hard work! Here's one they're gonna love!

1 cup sugar

1 cup creamy peanut butter (see Option)

1 egg

1 teaspoon vanilla extract

¼ cup mini M&Ms

1 Preheat the oven to 325°F. Coat an 8-inch square baking pan with nonstick cooking spray.

2 In a medium bowl, combine the sugar, peanut butter, egg, and vanilla. Add the M&Ms; mix well then press evenly into the baking pan.

3 Bake for 25 to 30 minutes, or until a wooden toothpick inserted in the center comes out clean. Allow to cool then cut into bars and serve.

Option: *If you want these to have extra-peanutty flavor, use crunchy peanut butter.*

162

Upside-Down Berry Cheesecake

Anybody can serve right-side-up cheese-cake. Only somebody really special would take a traditional dessert like cheesecake and turn it upside down . . . with such fantastic results! Give it a whirl and see for yourself!

SERVES 6 to 8

1. In a medium bowl, beat the heavy cream until stiff peaks form; set aside.

2. In a large bowl, beat the cream cheese until creamy. Add the pudding mix, milk, sugar, and lemon juice and continue beating until smooth.

3. Add the whipped cream and stir until well blended. Place the berries in a 9-inch pie plate. Spoon the cream cheese mixture over them and top with the crumbled graham crackers.

4. Serve, or cover and chill until ready to serve.

Preparation Tip: *For a quick-and-easy conventional fresh berry cheesecake, just spoon this cream cheese filling into a prepared 9-inch graham cracker pie crust and top with the berries.*

---

1 cup (½ pint) heavy cream

1 package (8 ounces) cream cheese, softened

1 package (4-serving size) vanilla instant pudding and pie filling mix

½ cup milk

2 tablespoons sugar

½ teaspoon lemon juice

1 pint fresh strawberries, washed, hulled, halved and patted dry *or* 1 pint fresh blueberries, washed and patted dry

4 graham crackers, crumbled

All-in-One Carrot Cake

SERVES 12 to 16

I was in a restaurant recently where I saw a mom desperately trying to get her son to eat some carrot sticks. I have a feeling he would have eaten his carrots this way. Do you think I could make it work with broccoli?

2 cups granulated sugar

1½ cups vegetable oil

4 eggs

2 teaspoons baking soda

2 cups all-purpose flour

2 teaspoons ground cinnamon

1 teaspoon salt

1 cup flaked coconut

3 cups grated carrots (about 1 pound carrots)

1 cup chopped walnuts

1 container (16 ounces) cream cheese frosting

1 Preheat the oven to 350°F. Coat a Bundt pan with nonstick cooking spray.

2 In a large bowl, combine all the ingredients except the frosting; blend with an electric beater until a smooth, thick batter forms. Pour the batter evenly into the Bundt pan.

3 Bake for 40 to 45 minutes, or until the top and sides are golden, and a wooden toothpick inserted in the center comes out clean.

4 Let cool completely then cover with the cream cheese frosting.

Preparation Tip: *To give this a light drizzle instead of covering it with frosting, remove the foil seal on the container of frosting and microwave the container for 30 to 60 seconds, or until pourable. Using a fork, drizzle the frosting over the cake.*

Kitchens are for Decorating

BY CAROL MCADOO REHME

To: *mom@email.mail*
From: *Katrina@email.mail*
Why does everyone suddenly think I need to learn how to cook? Just because I've got a husband now? Jason says a random sandwich or a bowl of cereal works fine for him.

BTW, my art classes are really paying off. Wish you could see what I've done with the apartment. Just have the kitchen left to do.

Late for class!

To: *Katrina@email.mail*
From: *mom@email.mail*
I e-mailed Kayla to suggest she share some of her recipes. Cooking doesn't have to be hard, you know. Your sister loves to cook.

How are you decorating the kitchen?

To: *mom@email.mail*
From: *Katrina@email.mail*
Kayla brought over meal menus and told me to plan ahead. LOL

She also brought a plastic zip bag of something called Amish Friendship Cake. After I make it, I'm supposed to pass along some of the cake, the recipe and part of the "starter" to someone else, kind of like an edible chain letter. Ever heard of it? You add ingredients and massage it. Or something like that. Gross. What a pain.

Wish you could see the kitchen! It's in my favorite yellows and blues. I even made a runner for the small table, collaged a wall hanging and painted a wooden shelf. I'm convinced—details make a difference.

Busy, busy!

To: *Katrina@email.mail*
From: *mom@email.mail*
I'm sure the kitchen is darling, but you can't live on love forever. Bet Jason would like to smell yummy things coming from it. Hint, hint.

What Kayla brought is sourdough starter. Your great-grandma once told me about sending her bread starter and a cake two miles down the road—an errand for one of her ten children—to her neighbor on baking day each week. Then her friend would tend it until her own baking day and send it back (along with some sourdough cake, I'm sure), shoe-leather-express, via a child from her own large brood. Do you suppose theirs was the first "friendship" cake?

Be sure you follow the directions!

To: *mom@email.mail*
From: *Katrina@email.mail*
Okay, so I didn't read all the directions.

Who knew that when the bag inflated like a balloon, you needed to "burp" it? While I was at class, it rolled right off the counter—and burst!

Milky and gaseous and growing. Fermented sourdough starter everywhere. Ugh. Ceiling, floor, rug, chair legs, tabletop, cabinets . . . no surface was safe.

You got your wish, Mom—here's definitely a smell to greet Jason when he comes home today. My cute kitchen is a mess!

FYI: I hate Friendship Cake.

To: *Katrina@email.mail*
From: *mom@email.mail*
As you said, details make a difference.

As soon as I quit laughing, I'll phone your sister. Maybe she'll help you clean up the mess.

Meanwhile, what are you planning for supper? :-)

Soda Pop Cake

SERVES 12 to 16

Lemon-lime soda like you've never tasted it before! This one's so easy to make and so much fun to serve, it'll be hard to keep your secret ingredient a secret!

1 package (18¼ ounces) lemon cake mix

1 egg

1 cup lemon-lime soda

Confectioners' sugar for topping

1. Preheat the oven to 350°F. Coat a 9" x 13" baking dish with nonstick cooking spray.

2. In a large bowl, combine all the ingredients except the confectioners' sugar; mix well and pour into the baking dish.

3. Bake for 30 to 35 minutes, or until a wooden toothpick inserted in the center comes out clean.

4. Let cool completely. Sprinkle with confectioners' sugar, cut into squares, and serve.

Serving Tip: *Garnish each cake square with a thin slice of lemon.*

Jazzy Bananas Foster

Longing for the flavor of this traditional New Orleans dessert? Just grab a skillet and you'll be on your way to some jazzy good taste mixed up right in your own kitchen.

SERVES 4 to 6

1. In a large skillet, melt the butter over medium heat. Add the brown sugar and cinnamon; stir until the sugar is melted.

2. Stir in the bananas and rum; cook for 2 to 3 minutes, or until heated through. Scoop the ice cream into serving bowls and top with the banana mixture. Serve immediately.

DID YOU KNOW . . . *that the average American consumes over 28 pounds of bananas each year? That must be why they're rated America's number 1 fruit!*

1/4 cup (1/2 stick) butter
1/2 cup packed brown sugar
1/8 teaspoon ground cinnamon
3 medium bananas, peeled and sliced
1/4 cup light or dark rum
1 quart vanilla ice cream

Healthy Hint:

Available all throughout the year, bananas are a great source of fiber, potassium, and Vitamin C, and contain no fat, cholesterol, or sodium. So, since they're so portable, they make a terrific take-along snack for us all.

THREE SCOOPS HIGH AND A ROLL OF FUN

BY JANET LYNN MITCHELL

It had been months since Marty and I had been on a date or did something fun with our kids. We accepted this reality, as our son Joel had been born prematurely. While he was still in the hospital, our kindergartner, Jenna Marie, was hospitalized with juvenile diabetes. Our past year had included thirteen hospitalizations and lots of stress, and we all braced ourselves for the next "whatever." We knew that somehow we needed to lighten the tension we all felt. We simply needed time with friends, and we needed to do something fun!

"I've got it!" I told Marty my idea, and with a wink of his eye and a nod of his head, I knew that he was game! Immediately, we called Jenna and Jason and shared the news.

"How would you like to have a slumber party?" Marty asked them after they ran in from outside. "A what?" Jason replied not having a clue what his father was talking about. "It's a sleepover party," I explained.

"A party?" Jenna shouted. "Yea, let's have a party!" Jason agreed while giving Jenna a high-five. Within minutes I was on the phone calling two of our friends to invite their kids to our family slumber party the next Friday night. "Look at it this way: We'll have your kids, and you guys can go out on a date!"

For the next few days, Marty, the kids, and I planned our slumber party. The kids' excitement was like electricity running through our home. Marty and I even had a sparkle in our eyes as we waited for the fun we knew we would have. Finally, it was Friday, and the kids arrived with sleeping bags in hand. Their parents were delighted they had the night off to have some extra fun themselves.

Marty helped the kids lay out their sleeping bags in the living room and then took them out to our backyard to play tag while I prepared the pizza. When dinner was ready, the kids found a seat at the "party table" and put on their party hats. Even Joel wore a hat. "We're celebrating everything!" Jennifer said.

170

"Tonight we're celebrating friends," I added.

Between bites of pizza, the kids giggled and told stories. Marty was the hit of the party, telling us every joke he knew. After dinner they watched a video while I cleaned up. When the movie ended, Marty scooped ice cream into bowls—three scoops high. He topped the ice cream with a generous helping of colored sprinkles and set the dishes on the table. Once the kids had happily devoured the dessert treat, Marty and I knew it was time. I gathered the "special decorations" we had set aside earlier and grabbed the video camera.

"Get your jackets," he instructed the kids. "We're going for a ride." Marty divided the kids, taking half in his car, while I took the others in my van. "Where are we going? What are we going to do?" echoed from the backseat. I could hardly contain my giggles but I didn't divulge the secret of where we were going and why.

"Hey, this is my house!" Matthew hollered as we drove by. I drove down the street and parked around the corner, followed by Marty.

"You're right. And we're about to decorate it!" I said.

The kids piled out and gathered around Marty and me. Opening the bags that we held, we handed each child a roll of toilet paper. "What are we going to do with this?" Jason asked, obliviously perplexed. "We're going to have some fun and decorate!" Marty announced. "Yep, we're going to surprise your parents and decorate your houses. You know, we'll wrap them like a present," I added.

Marty gave the instructions. "You can decorate the grass, trees and even the mailboxes. But when you see the lights of a car heading down the street, you either need to hit the ground, laying flat on the grass, or you can freeze in place, pretending you are a tree." The kids couldn't believe that we had planned something so outrageous, but when Marty gave the word, the decorating began. While the partiers toilet-papered Matthew's house, I videotaped the entire escapade. When we finished Matt's house, we headed off to house number two.

I wish we had been up early enough to see the faces of the surprised parents, but I can still hear the kids' laughter when we arrived the next morning to clean up after our fun. Once the yards were spotless, we gave each of the parents a videotape of our family slumber party, complete with ice cream sundaes—three scoops high—and their children acting like trees.

Family-Sized Sundae

This is a perfect treat to have on hand in the freezer when you want to get the family together around the table. Maybe you can make a deal with them before dinner: Eat all their veggies and you'll give 'em a big surprise for dessert! And, oh, will they be surprised by this!

½ gallon vanilla ice cream, divided

3 cups banana slices (3 medium bananas), divided

1 jar (12 ounces) hot fudge sauce, warmed to pourable consistency, divided

1 container (12 ounces) frozen whipped topping, thawed and divided

½ cup chopped walnuts, divided

⅔ cup maraschino cherries (about 24 cherries), divided

1. Scoop half of the ice cream into balls and place in the bottom of a large bowl or trifle dish. Layer with 1½ cups banana slices then spoon ½ cup of the hot fudge sauce over the bananas.

2. Spread half of the whipped topping over that. Sprinkle ¼ cup walnuts and ⅓ cup cherries on top. Repeat the layers then cover and freeze for at least 6 hours before serving.

3. Remove from the freezer 10 to 15 minutes before serving.

Preparation Tip: *By keeping certain items on hand in your pantry (and on your shopping list of "staples"), you're always sure to have what it takes to put together this fun family dessert!*

Apple-Blueberry Crunch

It used to be that moms would make dishes like this to use up an overabundance of a particular seasonal fruit. Now that we have ready access to all kinds of high-quality packaged frozen fruit, we can enjoy these comforting treats any time!

SERVES 12 to 15

1 Preheat the oven to 350°F. Coat a 9" x 13" baking dish with nonstick cooking spray.

2 Spread the apple pie filling over the bottom of the baking dish. In a medium bowl, combine the blueberries and sugar; spoon over the apple pie filling.

3 In another medium bowl, beat the cake mix with the water, oil, and egg whites until well combined. Spread the cake batter evenly over the blueberries and apples, and sprinkle with the walnuts.

4 Bake for 45 to 50 minutes, or until golden and bubbly.

1 can (21 ounces) apple pie filling

1 bag (14 ounces) frozen blueberries

¾ cup sugar

1 package (18¼ ounces) white cake mix

1 cup water

1 tablespoon vegetable oil

3 egg whites

1 cup walnuts, chopped

Garnishing Tip: *This is great served as is, or topped with ice cream and/or whipped cream.*

Did You Know. . . *that there's a whole bunch of cooked fruit desserts that are all just a bit different from each other? There are betties and brown betties, buckles, cobblers, crisps, crunches, crumbles, grunts, slumps, and don't forget pandowdies! All combine fruit with either dough, crumbs, or crumb topping, with granulated or brown sugar, and are cooked either in the oven or steamed. Give one a try when you're feeling fruity!*

173

Homemade Peanut Butter Cups

MAKES 12 TREATS

"Necessities" mean different things to different people. I know a few people who think chocolate is a true necessity. So for all those chocoholics, I created these jumbo peanut butter cups. They just might make it to your necessities list, too.

1 package (11 ½ ounces) milk chocolate chips, divided

3 tablespoons vegetable shortening, divided

1 ½ cups confectioners' sugar

1 cup creamy peanut butter

¼ cup (½ stick) butter, softened

1. Place paper baking cups into a 12-cup muffin tin.

2. In a small saucepan, melt 1 ¼ cups chocolate chips and 2 tablespoons shortening over low heat, stirring just until the mixture is smooth. Allow to cool slightly; the mixture should still be pourable.

3. Starting halfway up each paper cup, spoon about 2 teaspoons of the mixture over the inside of the cups, completely covering the bottom half of each cup. Chill the cups for about 30 minutes, until firm.

4. In a large bowl, combine the confectioners' sugar, peanut butter, and butter; mix well (mixture will by dry). Spoon equal amounts into the chocolate cups, pressing firmly.

5. Add the remaining ¾ cup chocolate chips and 1 tablespoon shortening to the saucepan and melt over low heat, stirring just until the mixture is smooth. Spoon equal amounts into the cups, spreading to completely cover the peanut butter mixture.

6. Cover and chill for at least 2 hours, or until firm.

THE FLOUR THAT HOLDS US TOGETHER

BY DEBI CALLIES

As a struggling single parent trying to salvage some sense of family tradition while working two jobs, raising four children and trying to complete a master's degree (in my spare time?), I was rushing to bake delectable goodies to hand out as presents for the holiday season that was quickly approaching.

Somehow my kitchen did not hold the same sense of tranquility and calm as my mother's did when she baked our family's traditional goodies. In trying to cram many days and hours of baking into one night, my kitchen was more like a tornado whirling in movement and action.

Of course, just as I was getting into a baking rhythm, I realized that my little bit of remaining flour would not be nearly enough to meet all my recipe's requirements. My oldest son, Bob, on holiday leave from the Marine Corps, had been an amused observer up to this point, but seeing me in distress, he volunteered to go to the store and buy some flour.

Perhaps there was an ulterior motive. Arriving home after his first deployment to the Iraq war, Bob had purchased his pride and joy: a 1974 blue Corvette. And I think the reality that evening was that he just wanted another excuse to drive it. There were times when I questioned who/what he missed more while he was away in Iraq: his mom or his Corvette?

Soon he returned from the store with the flour in hand—or, more

176

accurately, with the flour in his arms, for he had purchased a twenty-five-pound sack of it! I was speechless at first and just stood there with a funny look on my face. "Bob, how much baking do you think I am doing?" I asked. He just gave that special grin of his that melts my heart and said, "You didn't say how much."

Needless to say, all of our neighbors and loved ones received an additional gift of a few pounds of flour with their baked goodies that year.

Bob was only home for a short time before he had to return for a third deployment in Iraq. The days passed all too quickly as another Christmas season approached. I lacked all motivation to decorate the house and bake, yet I pushed ahead for the sake of my other children.

The house started to take shape as red, white and blue lights replaced the traditional red and green, inside and out. Another tradition remained—the baking and handing out of my mom's holiday cookies, many of which would be sent to Iraq.

I went to the store to purchase the needed ingredients. As always, pressed for time, I found myself racing down the aisles grabbing item after item until I came to the flour. I stopped. I stared at the flour. Suddenly, everything around me vanished, and I was transported back in time to the memory of Bob standing in our doorway with the sack of flour in his arms and that grin on his face. Tears rolled down my cheeks.

I froze unable to move and shake the memory. It was too hard. I wanted my son back from war and safe at home for Christmas. How could we celebrate and be joyful without him?

I started to turn and walk away without the flour, but then changed my mind. Somehow, this experience made me even more determined than ever to continue this family tradition. I couldn't give up on Christmas. More than parties and baked goods, Christmas is the love of family and God. It is the flour, the glue that holds us together during the tough times and allows us to laugh during the happier days for the love of family crosses oceans, deserts and even war zones.

Cappuccino Dessert

SERVES 4 to 6

Cappuccino has really become popular in this country in recent years. With this recipe, everybody-loves-it cappuccino is jumping out of the coffee cup and onto your dessert plate. *Delizioso!*

2 cups milk

2 tablespoons regular or decaffeinated instant coffee granules

1 package (4-serving size) instant chocolate pudding and pie filling

1½ cups frozen whipped topping, thawed

⅛ teaspoon ground cinnamon

1 In a large bowl, combine the milk and coffee granules. Add the pudding mix and beat with a wire whisk for 1 to 2 minutes, or until well blended. Reserve 2 tablespoons of the pudding in a medium bowl and divide the remaining pudding into 4 coffee cups or 4 to 6 individual glass dessert dishes.

2 Mix the whipped topping with the reserved pudding and spoon the topping mixture over the individual servings of pudding. Sprinkle the tops with the cinnamon and chill for at least 2 hours before serving.

Serving Tip: *To really fool your gang, make this dessert in glass coffee mugs. That way, they'll really think it's a cappuccino drink!*

Index

Who Is Mr. Food?

Art Ginsburg, better known as Mr. Food, has been a fixture on television news programs for more than twenty-five years.

Thanks to his regular presence in American homes via his TV spot syndicated by CBS/King World and seen by over 6 million viewers daily across the U.S., Mr. Food is widely recognized for his no-nonsense approach to food preparation. He consistently gives his loyal fans—from novices to experienced cooks—what they want: practical solutions to everyday mealtime dilemmas.

Mr. Food now also shares his quick-and-easy recipes and food tips on his daily radio show, which is distributed by Element One Networks, LLC, and heard on stations around the United States.

From his years of sharing "anybody can do it" recipes in various media, and as the author of more than forty cookbooks, Mr. Food knows that busy lifestyles require practical mealtime solutions, and he continues to offer creative ideas and fool-proof, tasty recipes that use only readily available ingredients.

In addition to this work prepared in conjunction with *Chicken Soup for the Soul*, Mr. Food has ongoing cookbook publishing relationships with Oxmoor House and the American Diabetes Association.

Mr. Food is continually making people's lives easier while finding fresh ideas for cooking up fun in the kitchen. The newest mealtime solutions from Mr. Food are his signature line of nonstick cookware and a chain of stores, Mr. Food no-fuss Meals, where guests assemble their own ready-to-cook meals using Mr. Food recipes and ingredients especially prepared by the Mr. Food no-fuss Meals team.

The well-known Mr. Food tagline, "OOH IT'S SO GOOD!!®", is one of a select number of sound marks registered by the U.S. Patent and Trademark Office.

For more quick 'n' easy Mr. Food recipes and tips, we invite you to visit *www.mrfood.com*.

Who Is Jack Canfield?

Jack Canfield is the co-creator and editor of the *Chicken Soup for the Soul*® series, which *Time* magazine has called "the publishing phenomenon of the decade." The series now has 105 titles with over 100 million copies in print in forty-one languages. Jack is also the co-author of eight other best-selling books including *The Success Principles™: How to Get from Where You Are to Where You Want to Be, Dare to Win, The Aladdin Factor, You've Got to Read This Book,* and *The Power of Focus: How to Hit Your Business, Personal and Financial Targets with Absolute Certainty.*

Jack has recently developed a telephone coaching program and an on-line coaching program based on his most recent book *The Success Principles.* He also offers a seven-day Breakthrough to Success seminar every summer, which attracts 400 people from fifteen countries around the world.

Jack is the CEO of Chicken Soup for the Soul Enterprises and the Canfield Training Group in Santa Barbara, California, and founder of the Foundation for Self-Esteem in Culver City, California. He has conducted intensive personal and professional development seminars on the principles of success for over 900,000 people in twenty-one countries around the world. He has spoken to hundreds of thousands of others at numerous conferences and conventions and has been seen by millions of viewers on national television shows such as *The Today Show, Fox and Friends, Inside Edition, Hard Copy,* CNN's *Talk Back Live, 20/20, Eye to Eye,* and the *NBC Nightly News* and the *CBS Nightly News.*

Jack is the recipient of many awards and honors, including three honorary doctorates and a Guinness World Records Certificate for having seven *Chicken Soup for the Soul* books appearing on the *New York Times* bestseller list on May 24, 1998.

To write to Jack or for inquiries about Jack as a speaker, his coaching programs or his seminars, use the following contact information:

Jack Canfield
The Canfield Companies
P.O. Box 30880, Santa Barbara, CA 93130
phone: 805-563-2935 • Fax: 805-563-2945
E-mail: *info@jackcanfield.com* • Web site: *www.jackcanfield.com*

Who Is Mark Victor Hansen?

In the area of human potential, no one is more respected than Mark Victor Hansen. For more than thirty years, Mark has focused solely on helping people from all walks of life reshape their personal vision of what's possible. His powerful messages of possibility, opportunity and action have created powerful change in thousands of organizations and millions of individuals worldwide.

He is a sought-after keynote speaker, bestselling author and marketing maven. Mark's credentials include a lifetime of entrepreneurial success and an extensive academic background. He is a prolific writer with many best-selling books such as *The One Minute Millionaire, The Power of Focus, The Aladdin Factor and Dare to Win,* in addition to the *Chicken Soup for the Soul* series. Mark has made a profound influence through his library of audios, videos and articles in the areas of big thinking, sales achievement, wealth building, publishing success, and personal and professional development.

Mark is also the founder of MEGA Seminar Series. MEGA Book Marketing University and Building Your MEGA Speaking Empire are annual conferences where Mark coaches and teaches new and aspiring authors, speakers and experts on building lucrative publishing and speaking careers. Other MEGA events include MEGA Marketing Magic and My MEGA Life. He has appeared on television (*Oprah,* CNN and *The Today Show*), in print (*Time, U.S. News & World Report, USA Today, New York Times* and *Entrepreneur*) and on countless radio interviews, assuring our planet's people that, "You can easily create the life you deserve."

As a philanthropist and humanitarian, Mark works tirelessly for organizations such as Habitat for Humanity, American Red Cross, March of Dimes, Childhelp USA and many others. He is the recipient of numerous awards that honor his entrepreneurial spirit, philanthropic heart and business acumen. He is a lifetime member of the Horatio Alger Association of Distinguished Americans, an organization that honored Mark with the prestigious Horatio Alger Award for his extraordinary life achievements.

Mark Victor Hansen & Associates, Inc.
P.O. Box 7665, Newport Beach, CA 92658
phone: 949-764-2640 • fax: 949-722-6912
Visit Mark online at: *www.markvictorhansen.com*

Contributors

If you would like to contact any of the contributors for information about their writing or to invite them to speak in your community, look for their contact information included in their biographies.

Linda Apple and her husband Neal live in northwest Arkansas. Four of their five children are married. They have two grandchildren and are expecting another in September. Thankfully, Neal finally discovered his culinary talents and now helps Linda in the kitchen during the holidays. Contact Linda at *psalm10218@cox.net; www.lindacapple.com*.

Jean Blackmer is co-author of *Where Women Walked: Powerful True Stories of Women, Perseverance and God's Provision.* She is currently writing a book about mothering boys and is seeking humorous stories and anecdotes. She can be reached via e-mail at *jean@rockrimmon.net.* She lives in Boulder, Colorado, with her husband and three sons.

Jean Brody writes a weekly newspaper column and a monthly magazine column. This is her ninth story in *Chicken Soup* publications. Her short stories and poetry have appeared in many anthologies, and she's won a number of awards for her work. Jean lives in Kentucky with her husband and cat.

Debi Callies is the author of *Stay Strong, Stay Safe My Son,* a book describing her challenges in sending her son Robert to war. Debi is also the proud mother of three other children: Demi, Kaila and Drew. Please e-mail her at *vpmm@cox.net*.

M. Mylene English delivers her sometimes quirky, sometimes irreverent views with honesty and humor in her newspaper column, "It'll BE Fine." An *It'll BE Fine* anthology was published in 2002. Mylene's work has appeared in *Reader's Digest, Our Canada, Chicken Soup for the Mother and Daughter Soul* and *Chicken Soup for the Mother and Son Soul.* Mylene lives in northern Alberta with her husband and five children. Please contact Mylene at *wordsmith@echoecho.ca* or visit *www.echoecho.ca*

Caryl Ginsburg Fantel enjoys her "never a dull moment" life with her husband and two daughters. She juggles her career as V.P. of Publishing and Communications for Mr. Food (who happens to be her dad) with her avocation of pianist/musical director and involvement in numerous community service organizations. Caryl can be contacted at *info@mrfood.com*.

Debbie Farmer writes the award-winning syndicated column "Family Daze." Her book *Don't Put Lipstick on the Cat* is available online or in bookstores. When not busy writing or being a mom, Debbie is either teaching first grade, shoe shopping or meeting friends for coffee. For information on having "Family Daze" appear in your newspaper, e-mail *familydaze@home.com* or visit the Family Daze Web site at *www.familydaze.com*.

Marian Gormley is a freelance writer and photographer who has been published in regional, national and international publications, including *Chicken Soup for Every Mom's Soul.* She has a background in software engineering, public relations and marketing. Residing with her family in Virginia, she writes primarily about parenting, family life, education, health and the arts.

Anneliese Homan received her Bachelor's degree from Southwestern College, and her Master's and Education Specialist degrees from Central Missouri State University. She is a community college English teacher as well as a freelance writer. In addition to traveling and working with her students she enjoys hiking the Katie Trail with her husband and their golden retriever Daisy. Please e-mail her at *ahoman@sfccmo.edu*.

Ellen Javernick is a busy mother and grandmother who lives in Loveland, Colorado. She teaches first grade and especially enjoys working with struggling students. She is the author of sixteen books and articles for numerous magazines. You can e-mail her at *javernicke@aol.com*.

Maureen Johnson has been previously published in the *Chicken Soup* series. She is currently working with an editor on a Young Adult manuscript. Maureen lives in Sydney, Australia. She teaches high school, writes and never bakes cookies with her son, Paddy, who thinks she's the worst baker in the world. E-mail her at *macbethm@optus.net.*

Jaye Lewis is an award-winning writer who, at age sixty, still finds motherhood the most important, funny and rewarding job she has ever had. You can read more of Jaye's inspirational stories on her Web site at *www.entertainingangels.org* or e-mail Jaye at *jayelewis@comcast.net.*

Barbara LoMonaco received her Bachelor of Science degree from the University of Southern California and taught elementary school. Barbara has worked for *Chicken Soup for the Soul* since February 1998 as their Story Acquisitions Manager and their Customer Service representative. She is a co-author of *Chicken Soup for the Mother and Son Soul.* Contact Barbara at *blomonaco@chickensoupforthesoul.com.*

Janet Lynn Mitchell is a wife, mother of three, author and inspirational speaker. Her books, *A Special Kind of Love, Hands-On Faith—Family Nights* and *Hands-On Faith—Family Fun* are now available. Watch for her book, Taking a Stand, published by Green Key Books, to be released in October 2006. Contact Janet at *Janetlm@prodigy.net.*

Maryjo Faith Morgan loves getting up just to write each day. She has published stories in other *Chicken Soup* editions, magazine articles on a wide variety of topics, and in Cup of Comfort. An avid reader, she enjoys hiking and tandem biking in Colorado. Please visit *www.maryjofaith morgan.com.*

Ann Morrow and her family live in Custer, South Dakota, where she writes humor/inspirational pieces. She plans to continue making people smile through her newspaper columns, future books and possible syndication. Please e-mail Ann at *nova@gwtc.net* or visit her Web site at *www.ann morrow.com.*

Carol McAdoo Rehme, one of *Chicken Soup's* most prolific authors, claims motherhood as her most important calling. Once "mommy" to four preschoolers, she is now "grammy" to three . . . and finds herself—once again—in the kitchen. Carol directs the non-profit Vintage Voices, Inc., which makes interactive arts programs to the frail elderly. Contact her at *carol@rehme.com; www. rehme.com.*

Harriet May Savitz is the award-winning author of twenty-four books, including *Is a Worry Worrying You?* (Tanglewood Press picture book) co-authored with Ferida Wolff. Reissued books by AuthorsGuild/iUniverse about the disabled can be found at *www.iUniverse.com* and *www. harrietmaysavitz.com* or contact her at *hmaysavitz@aol.com.*

Cristy Trandahl has been a teacher and a writer for the nation's leading student progress monitoring company. Today she home-educates her six children at their home in rural Minnesota. Cristy has contributed to the bestselling *Cup of Comfort* series and various regional anthologies. Please e-mail her at *davecristy@frontiernet.net.*

June Williams lives in Brush Prairie, Washington, with her husband Mac. She enjoys baking, reading, camping and spending lots of time with her grandchildren.

Robin Ehrlichman Woods uses her experience as a mother, teacher and community activist to write personal experience and humor essays for online and print publications. She has recently expanded her horizons by writing in the romance genre and continues to be a weirdly creative cook.

Permissions *(continued from page ii)*

Rainy Day Rescue. Reprinted by permission of June Williams. ©2005 June Williams.

Please Pass the Feelings. Reprinted by permission of Marian Gormley. ©1999 Marian Gormley.

Bad (Pot) Luck. Reprinted by permission of Robin Ehrlichman Woods. ©2005 Robin Ehrlichman Woods.

Ketchup with Kids. Reprinted by permission of Cristy Trandahl. ©2006 Cristy Trandahl.

My Sous-Chef. Reprinted by permission of Marian Gormley. ©1996 Marian Gormley.

My Culinary Epiphany. Reprinted by permission of Linda Apple. ©2005 Linda Apple.

The Latkes Epidemic. Reprinted by permission of Harriet May Savitz. ©2005 Harriet May Savitz.

The Plate Made the Meal. Reprinted by permission of Maryjo Faith Morgan. ©2006 Maryjo Faith Morgan.

The Secret Ingredient. Reprinted by permission of Jean Brody. ©2006 Jean Brody.

Nothing to Share. Reprinted by permission of Maryjo Faith Morgan. ©2006 Maryjo Faith Morgan.

Where's The Turkey? Reprinted by permission of Barbara LoMonaco. ©2006 Barbara LoMonaco.

Pantry Panache. Reprinted by permission of Carol McAdoo Rehme. ©2006 Carol McAdoo Rehme.

My Trusted, Crusty Friend. Reprinted by permission of Anneliese Homan. ©2006 Anneliese Homan.

Without a Tail. Reprinted by permission of Maureen Johnson. ©2005 Maureen Johnson.

Kitchens Are for Decorating. Reprinted by permission of Carol McAdoo Rehme. ©2006 Carol McAdoo Rehme.

Three Scoops High and a Roll of Fun. Reprinted by permission of Janet Lynn Mitchell. ©2005 Janet Lynn Mitchell.

The Flour That Holds Us Together. Reprinted by permission of Debi Callies. ©2005 Debi Callies.